Manage *the* Gap

Achieving Success with Intergenerational Teams

Steve Butler

R3THINK PRESS

First published in Great Britain in 2019 by Rethink Press (www.rethinkpress.com)

To my wife, Elizabeth, for her loving support.

To Jonathan, Angus and Kenneth, who have entrusted me with the leadership of their latest growth stage venture.

To my children, Ellen, Bethany, Hannah and George, and my stepchildren, Olivia, Emily and Sylvie, who are a constant inspiration to me and have endeavoured to teach me the language of Generation Z.

Contents

Introduction

Planning your company's future? Then this book is for you.

Look around you – at the employees sharing your office, milling about and grabbing coffee. What age range are they in? Now think forward ten or fifteen years. You're that much older... and so are they.

Imagine that there are fewer people in their twenties and thirties sitting at those desks. There are also far more people in their fifties and sixties, and a few in their seventies. How would that affect the dynamics in your business? How might you need to change the design of your workplace, or your management structure?

That shift in age ranges is a reflection of our changing society: the inevitable outcome of changes in our country's demographics. Put simply, fewer young people will be entering the workforce in the next couple of decades – and retaining them in an increasingly competitive market presents a major challenge. On the other hand, many more people at the other end of the conveyor belt will be wanting or needing to stay economically active – and you'll be needing them too.

Over the last few years, businesses have had to navigate a revolution in technology that has utterly transformed the workplace. Now another revolution is underway: a demographic one. Unless you're on the cusp of the curve, you and your company run the risk of emulating one of the 'dinosaur' businesses that failed to grasp the competitive advantages of technology and sank without trace.

Dealing with these changes will be challenging for business managers. Different generations bring with them different skills, assets and attitudes towards work. How will that change the way you manage your staff? How will it affect the training you give them, the benefits you offer, the hours you ask them to work, and the way they should work together?

For the last few years, I've been wrestling with the challenges of merging workforces and creating project teams. This has meant harnessing the talents of people from different generations and mindsets. If you get this right, you can build a powerful team of people who are motivated, loyal, productive and innovative. Get it wrong, and you'll be trying to herd cats.

Are you ready to deal with those issues and turn a business weakness into a strength – a business threat into an opportunity? This book is about what I've learned from experience (through trial and error) and what I've gleaned from the ways in which forward-looking companies around the world are tackling the issue. If you're a manager in a small or medium enterprise (SME) and you're wondering how to get the best out of the people who work for you – whatever their age – then this book is for you.

It's the book I wish someone had written for me to read five years ago.

Why we need to look again at our working lives

Before I reached the age of thirty, I had sold life insurance at the dockside to soldiers who were leaving Portsmouth for the first Gulf War, convinced the owners of a flip-flop factory in Nairobi to sign over their profits to a large insurer to invest on their behalf, cold-called Uruguay's finance minister to ask for a meeting (I got it) and set out on my first attempt to climb (part of) Mount Everest. Before I turned forty, the investment performance assessment company I founded had been bought by one of the UK's best-known institutional pension investment specialists. I now lead more than one hundred and fifty people in a multi-million-pound turnover pensions and investments business, overseeing four billion pounds' worth of assets. These experiences have shaped me – and the way I approach work.

Then there are the personal factors that play a part in how I look at the world: married for the second time, I'm a father of four and a stepdad of three. My own, natural father is a distant figure; if he taught me one thing, it is not to be that. Every one of my colleagues, contacts and friends has their own story to share, and anyone who is passionate about building a business needs to hear them. We might be at different milestones but we're all heading for the same destination: the era of age diversity. The world of work – how it is carried out, and by whom – is rapidly morphing into a maelstrom of technological, social and cultural change, sucking in everything within reach. Understanding the dynamics of those changes will be critical for every business leader if they are to succeed in the coming decades.

Armed with an MBA, a part-completed doctorate in age diversity, thirty years in financial services leadership and (some say) a masochist's desire to not just walk on by, I want to explore how, together, we can respond to this transformation in the core human experience: our working lives. So, just before I turn fifty, I have set myself another task: to navigate what will be one of the twenty-first century's defining issues. This book is the first leg of that journey.

What our children can teach us about age diversity at work

Having four children and three stepchildren, all now in their late teens and early twenties, has given me a vision of what the future workplace could be like. Believe me, it's going to be complicated.

Watching them talk with their friends about starting their careers has been a real eye-opener – although perhaps I should rephrase that. Even though the older ones are in their early twenties, they're not really thinking about starting careers at all. They've all been to uni. Some are now doing a second degree, even if they're not particularly academic. Their reasoning seems to amount to: 'Why not?' Others are planning to travel or spend a couple of years working shifts in a pub or hipster coffee bar before they get a job they really want. And while what they earn when they do start their proper career matters, it's not the big driver that it was for my generation. Their mindset isn't: 'we need to get a good job to get on to the housing ladder'. Instead, it's 'we want to do something that offers a good work-life balance and can make a positive social difference'.

I don't mean to sound like an old fuddy-duddy, but it wasn't like that in my day. Everyone I knew finished their A levels or degrees and started submitting CVs. Once you got your foot in the door, you put your head down and tried to work your way up.

The conversations my children and their mates are having are being replicated up and down the country… just one sign of a profound change happening in the workplace.

This is a change that, as an employer, is on my mind. It's one that I believe we all should be talking about much more. As we live longer, people's work patterns are shifting – and they'll continue to shift. My children's generation knows that they might well live into their eighties, nineties or even beyond one hundred. The way things are going, they might be working, in some form or another, until they are octogenarians. So what's the rush to get started? Taking longer breaks from work – to care for relatives or fulfil other ambitions – may also be an option. How does that fit in with the conventional career ladder?

As a CEO, I look at my family and wonder whether, in a few years' time, we are going to have trouble recruiting good young people. I also wonder what the other implications might be for our workforces, with people starting work later in life and staying in work for many years longer.

In some industries, there already appears to be a hiring crunch. Anecdotal evidence suggests, for example, that a huge proportion of financial advisers are in their fifties or older, with a shortage of young people joining the profession. Of course, industry-specific reasons may be contributing to this, but I see it as part of a wider trend. Meanwhile, at the other end of the spectrum, people are already working for much longer than they used to. Retirement ages are inching ever upwards, driven by government poli-cies, economic needs and better health. Many people never really retire at all. As an employer, that throws up challenges – not least, how you manage the gap between the different expectations and needs of these generations. But it also creates opportunities.

As my own company has grown and we have hired or otherwise brought more employees under our umbrella, I've come to realise that these issues are not theoretical. They're real, they're happening now, and they need to be tackled.

My lightbulb moment

One of the key messages in this book is: if you're going to manage an age-diverse workforce, and if you want get the most out of them, then you need to acknowledge how the mindsets and life experiences of different generations affect the way they approach their work, and how they work together.

The story of John and Johanna

They are two real people in my office, both of whom are happy to be included here. John is an archetypal Baby Boomer in his early fifties; Johanna is in her twenties and as Millennial as you can get. Both are hugely talented and lovely people, whose skills I need to make my business work. But when it comes to the workplace, they are as alike as chalk and cheese... though a better analogy might be oil and water – or gunpowder and matches.

The story starts three years ago: after about fifteen years of building up my own retirement savings business, I was approached by the investor behind my company, Punter Southall, to come under their wing and lead an exciting new venture in the retirement savings sector. It was a big career move for me. And a challenge. For a start, I was moving from a company of just twenty-five people to one projected to be several hundred strong within a few years.

As you do in these situations, my first thought was: 'I can't do this on my own... I need a few good people around me I can rely on.' My first port of call was John, with whom I'd worked twenty-five years ago. John had spent a long and successful career in business development and marketing – key aspects of building up a new venture from scratch. I saw him as a lieutenant and friend in this business, as well as a safe pair of hands. I haven't been disappointed.

I suppose you'd describe John as 'old school'. He comes to work dressed smartly, gets in on time, likes his own desk and carries himself as someone who has been around the block more than once. Importantly, although the world of sales and marketing have changed fundamentally since we both set out in the pre-internet world, John has kept pace with the changes. He has a set of skills and an understanding of the financial services market that I value enormously.

Now let's turn to Johanna.

Some eighteen months ago, a CV landed on my desk like I'd never seen before. For a start it was all bright colours, so I could hardly miss it. It didn't tell me much about her, which I would have expected a CV to do. It wasn't even in response to a job advert. Instead, it told me all about her skill set and what she was going to do to transform my business – and, in fairness, she had obviously done her homework.

I thought: 'I must see this person.'

Johanna came in, and her presence lived up to her letter. She had a detailed awareness of my business, and she delivered a compelling and eloquent presentation about what she could do for me, and what support she'd need to achieve that. She was a real force to be reckoned with and I came away thinking, 'Well, I don't have a vacancy for that person – but I want her in the company.'

Johanna is a classic Millennial. She doesn't do the nine to five, but she's still emailing me with ideas at eleven o'clock at night. She's happiest not at her desk but slouched on a sofa with her laptop and her headphones on, nibbling peanuts. She wants the business to have a mission. She thrives on teamwork and collaboration. She craves feedback – and for me to tell her how she's doing. She flouts all management structure and comes to me all the time to give her direction and talk about next steps.

That's just the way she is. And if I want her in my team, that's what I have to accept.

Because of their complementary skills, I thought that putting Johanna and John in a project team would be dynamite. 'They're going to do wonderful things,' I fondly imagined.

Six months afterwards, an opportunity came along to do just that... and, yes, it was explosive. But not in a good way. Within a week, they had both asked to speak privately to me. 'I can't work with her/him.' 'He/she has no respect for me.' 'She doesn't appreciate my experience and all that I've done.' 'He's set in his ways and won't give me the freedom to do things.'

Like I said, oil and water.

It rapidly reached the point where both said they couldn't work with the other – and I had to step in to coach and mentor them through to the end of the project. If I'm honest, although they do get on better now, there is still this friction between them. If I put them together, I have to actively manage that rub.

It's a classic example of different generations coming to work with different attitudes and mindsets. Neither is going to change that much, because they have default settings on certain things, so we have to find workarounds that make it possible for them to collaborate.

My approach

If you're handling a management team with two individuals like John and Johanna in it – admittedly extreme examples of the generational divide – you need to manage their individual requirements. They need different things from you as a manager, and if you want them in your team, it's up to you to provide them.

One of the problems is their varying perspectives on the concept of structure – or hierarchy.

John's been brought up in a highly structured world where you started at the bottom and worked your way up, and where seniority demanded respect. Johanna simply looks at what a person brings to a project in terms of ideas, not necessarily how many years they've served. And she's not afraid to say it how it is. John makes judgements, based on decades of experience, on what will work and what won't. Johanna is looking to break the mould: her generation are constantly reinventing their world and they aren't keen on convention for convention's sake.

Both of these approaches have merit. So how do we deal with these differences to get the best out of both of them? How do we ally Johanna's ambition and irreverent enthusiasm with John's knowledge and sound experience? My solution was to set out terms of reference, or 'terms of engagement', in a much more detailed way than I've ever had to do before.

In my company, especially in marketing, work is done on a project basis. That means we don't have a hierarchy but a pretty flat structure. So, the 'terms of engagement' between the two of them are these: we set out what John brings to a project and what we expect him to deliver; we find out that Johanna brings other things, and this is what we expect from her; and when we do have conflicts, this is how we're going to deal with it. And if we can't agree, then I have the final say.

For example, the project I had put them together on was a research report. John had a particular idea on how it should be presented, and Johanna had another (radically different) one. Because John had spent a lifetime in marketing, he understood the value of the brand and wanted to stick to it. To that, Johanna simply said, 'Phoo. It needs to engage the recipient and ram home the key points… brand is less important for this project.'

No one is right all the time; and, in this instance, I had to step back and consider the reader of the report. I then had to get John to understand that if we did go off-brand a little, nothing bad would happen; while encouraging Johanna to understand that there is value in being on-brand because it fits into a bigger picture. In effect, this was a compromise that pushed the brand in a sparky and engaging way, and achieved the best of all worlds.

And what happened with this project? Yes, there were some cross words and dented egos. And yes, it took an inordinate amount of management time to get sorted. But it was worth it: it led directly to a series of highly successful seminars and a lot of new business. By coincidence, when Johanna and I sat down together recently she told me that she'd been reading my blogs on this topic – and, as a result, now understands more of John's perspective. John? Well, he's mellowed a bit too.

And the moral of this tale?

As a manager, it's not just about being there as a hand on someone's shoulder when things go awry. It's also about anticipating the potential for discord, proactively working out what each employee needs, and treating them as individuals. That's light years from how managers managed when I started work, but that's how it is.

In my workforce (and probably yours) there are also Generation X and Generation Z team members to worry about – all of them with different needs and expectations, and the potential to cause friction with other employees. To get the most out of each of them, you need to recognise the dynamic of the relationships between them and navigate ways in which they can work together. If you can do that, you will stand a chance of achieving success with intergenerational teams.

PART ONE

UNDERSTAND THE GAP

ONE

The Changing Landscape Of The Workplace

Time to change

There's no question that our workforce is ageing. That reflects the population as a whole: life expectancy has moved up markedly in recent decades. In 1951, women in England and Wales could expect (on average) to live to the age of seventy-two and men to sixty-six. By 2011, women were living to the age of eighty-three and men to seventy-nine. Since then, the figure has actually dipped slightly (ONS, 2015) – but the message is clear: we're living longer.

We're also working longer. In the UK, 30% of the workforce is already over the age of fifty, and the number of people between the ages of sixty-five and sixty-nine who are working doubled between 2001 and 2014 (Lain

& Loretto, 2016). All this at a time when the upcoming generation of 'worker bees' are starting their careers later because more are going through higher education: up to 49.8% in the 2016/2017 academic year compared with 41.7% ten years before. Go back a further twenty years to the late 1980s, and the percentage of young people going to college and university was around 15%. It is no longer the norm to start working at eighteen and retire at sixty-five (Dearing, 1997).

UK employment rate by age group, 1998–2018 (ONS, 2017)

Age (years)	People in employment (%)		
	1998	2008	2018
16 to 17	48	33	26
18 to 24	67	64	62
25 to 34	78	81	83
35 to 49	81	83	85
50 to 64	59	66	72
65 and over	5	7	10

This is a major shift: as our pre-work lives have extended, so have our working lives. One reason is that because we are living longer (and enjoying more healthy years of life), we need to fund longer retirements. But recent studies suggest other factors are at work as well. Although life expectancy has increased for people in all age groups, the improvements are far more marked for those in higher socio-economic groups. That's reflected in working longevity: employees who are educated to a higher level are more likely to prolong their working life (Angeloni & Borgonovi, 2016). So are those who are healthier (Patrickson & Ranzijn, 2004). And as companies adapt to this new reality by giving older staff more support, those same staff are likely to stay employed for longer (Radford & Chapman, 2015).

The following table shows where the working population will be coming from in the next few decades. This makes clear that if employers want to be able to take on the staff they need to keep their wheels turning, they will have to employ more older people.

Projected age distribution of UK population, 1975–2045 (ONS, 2017)

Year	UK population	0 to 15 years (%)	16 to 64 years (%)	65 years and over (%)
1975	56,226,000	24.9	61.0	14.1
1985	56,554,000	20.7	64.1	15.2
1995	58,025,000	20.7	63.4	15.8
2005	60,413,000	19.3	64.7	15.9
2015	65,110,000	18.8	63.3	17.8
2025	69,444,000	18.9	60.9	20.2
2035	73,044,000	18.1	58.3	23.6
2045	76,055,000	17.7	57.8	24.6

For international evidence, just look at countries like Japan, which has an even bigger 'Baby Boomer bump' and markedly slowing birth rates. They are already making the adjustments needed to cope with an ageing workforce. According to the World Economic Forum (2019), 'as many as 12 million Japanese people may disappear from the country's workforce by 2040. That's a fall of around 20%'. Japan's approach has been to encourage more women into the workplace in senior roles (an area where Japan is behind many Western countries) and to support and encourage more older people to stay in work.

And there's more. In their article 'How work will change when most of us live to 100', expert authors on this topic Lynda Gratton and Andrew Scott (2016) propose that people will not only start work later, but may change career several times during their longer working lives. That too has major implications for companies who looking to recruit and retain talented people.

The impact of legislation and policy

Alongside these demographic changes, several major pieces of legislation that have been introduced over the last few years have also altered the landscape. For decades, it was the custom that companies looking to cut costs would show the door to workers well before they reached State Pension age. More recently, the government has recognised that keeping older people in the workforce is actually a good thing.

First, the UK Government brought in the Employment Equality Age Regulations (DTI, 2006), which prohibited employers from unreasonably discriminating against employees because of their age. Then, in 2011, the Department for Work and Pensions went one further and abolished the default retirement age. Employers could no longer force workers to retire at age sixty-five unless they could justify it. In the same year, the government (ONS, 2016) moved the 'goalposts' for retirement to make the State Pension age equal for men and women at age sixty-five by 2019, and then increase it to age sixty-six by 2020. This means a large group (2.6 million) of women born in the 1950s onwards are retiring later than they had expected to. The government is also planning to raise the State Pension age from sixty-six to sixty-seven between 2026 and 2028.

On top of this, the Pension Taxation Act (HMRC, 2014) allows individuals to access their pension pots on a more flexible basis from age fifty-five, giving them more freedom to adjust their working lives.

Pensions change plans

All these changes have had a significant impact on employees' working lives – as well as their plans for the future. A survey carried out by the Chartered Institute of Personnel and Development (CIPD, 2014), the professional body for human resources (HR) and people development, suggested that 54% of employees intend to work beyond the age of sixty-five.

Research published by my own company, Punter Southall Aspire, in June 2018 (Nelson, 2018) shows that one-fifth of people who have officially retired are still working on a part-time or casual basis. Among those who have not retired yet, 43% said they plan to retire before they turn sixty-five and another 17% plan to retire fully before the age of seventy.

If a growing workforce of over-seventies sounds far-fetched, according to ONS figures (Hill, 2019) nearly one in nine men aged seventy or over are already working full or part time. That's an increase of 137% over the past ten years. The number of women aged seventy or over and still working has also more than doubled in that time: 175,000 are in work, which is an increase of 131%.

While better health in later life may explain this in part, financial expediency is also a factor. This will only increase as another significant trend works its way through the system: the number of companies offering 'gold plated' defined benefit (DB) pensions for their employees is rapidly withering. Some industry experts are predicting that the number of these plans available will shrink by a further 80% in the next quarter of a century (Pension Policy Institute, 2016). Many more employees are now starting to put money into their pension pots via auto-enrolment, which is a government initiative that requires every employer to put their staff into a workplace pension and to make contributions towards their employee's pension. This is still at levels well below what any pensions adviser would say is enough for a financially secure retirement. The new State Pension (at around £8,000 a year) is merely a safety net. That means a large section of the population – many of whom will not have property wealth to fall back on – will simply need to keep on working for longer, especially if they want to afford a decent level of care in their later years.

Too many older people are still economically inactive when they'd prefer to be earning a crust but the trends all point to more of them staying in jobs or returning to the workforce. Figures released by the CIPD (2019) showed that the number of people in work had increased by 457,000 over the previous year, and that more than 70% were aged fifty or older. In response to those figures, the CIPD (2019) issued this statement:

It's not entirely clear why certain groups have benefited from the extraordinary strong employment growth over the past year. Changing demographics is undoubtedly a factor, but another possibility is that employers are being forced to widen their recruitment channels and make work more accessible in response to the tightening labour market.

The good news for businesses is that although the number of younger people coming into the world (and the workforce) is reducing, the number of older people available for work – who are healthy enough to do it *and* keen to get paid – is on the rise. Those people are a resource to be tapped into.

The conundrum is how to make sure that the older people you do recruit, retain and retrain blend smoothly with the rest of your workforce. That's what the rest of this book will help you to do.

KEY POINTS

1. Because of changing demographics, if employers are going to be able to maintain their workforce into the future, they will have to recruit, retain or retrain more older people.

2. Growing numbers of those in their sixties, seventies and even beyond are looking to remain in the workforce – either through choice or financial necessity.

3. A large number are keen to work part rather than full time in order to combine caring duties or to 'wind down' by taking on less onerous roles.

4. Improving health among large numbers of older people means that they are more than capable of being high-functioning employees.

5. The challenge for businesses is how to make sure that the older people they recruit, retain and retrain blend smoothly with the rest of their workforce.

TWO

The Analogue Generations

Five generations

The premise of this book is that the workplace, like society itself, comprises different generations of people – and, ideally, we all need to find the best ways of collaborating.

Each generation has been shaped by the cultural, historical, political, educational and economic influences that prevailed, and by the major events that took place, while they were growing up. As a result, each generation approaches life and work in its own distinct way.

To harness all that these cohorts can bring to the workplace, you need to understand how they were moulded, what their priorities in life are, and what will motivate them to give of their best. If you have the time and patience, you'll find reams of worthy research to plough through. But if you're a busy CEO, is there a more direct way to understand this whole 'generation gap' issue? Nothing involving people is ever simple, but we can make some broad observations and assumptions.

Let's start with how the generations are traditionally divided:

THE FIVE GENERATIONS

The Silent Generation. Born between 1926 and 1945, they are hardworking, dedicated and dutiful. They are now largely out of the world of work (although Warren Buffett, Carlos Slim and Larry Ellison are notable exceptions), so we will put them to one side for the purposes of this book.

The Baby Boomers. Born between 1946 and 1964, during a time of increasing prosperity, upward social mobility and the crumbling of longstanding mores. This period was also marked by a 'boom' in the number of children who were born and survived infancy.

Generation X. Born between 1965 and 1980 into a time of major cultural and technological change. This generation was influenced by the turbulent economics of the late seventies and eighties, and by wider access to further education.

Millennials (or Generation Y). Born between 1980 and the mid-1990s, a time of rising aspirations and digital innovation. The children of the Baby Boomers, this generation in particular has been affected by the recent decade of austerity.

Generation Z. Born from the late 1990s onwards, this generation is now starting to enter work. They are true 'digital natives'. Often unkindly characterised as 'snowflakes', they are beginning to make their voices heard on the planet they are soon to inherit.

Sweeping assumptions have been made about how each of these generations sees the world, but some caution is required. Recent research (Parry & Urwin, 2017) argues that generational differences cannot readily by grouped by year of birth; people need to be categorised by experience rather than age, unless research data is statistically large enough to overcome all other characteristics. In other words, what has shaped a person individually (for example, their education, family or social class) may have as much say in determining their character as what was going on at the time they grew up.

Does that undermine generational characterisations? Not quite. Enough studies have been done, and enough reliable observations have been made by managers from inside a multitude of workplaces, to prove that statistics do support some broad(ish) assumptions – while recognising that there can be employees who will not readily fit into a conveniently shaped jelly mould. No generation can remain unaffected by the significant events and cultural influences of the time, whether that's Watergate, 9/11, austerity or Brexit; they are not just affected by how their parents raised them.

In terms of differentiating population cohorts, though, there is one huge change which has affected us all – and in different ways. That change is information technology: IT. People in Generation X (like me), along with the Boomer generation, have come to terms with and largely embraced the evolution of IT in the workplace. For younger people, though, IT was part of their lives from much earlier – at school and at home.

If you want to define a single rift that divides us, it is the post-1980 Digital generations compared with the preceding Analogue ones.

Characterising the Analogue generations

Baby Boomers: 1946–1964

Famous Boomers

Tim Berners-Lee, Tony Blair, David Bowie, Richard Branson, Hillary Clinton, Princess Diana, Bill Gates, Steve Jobs, Cath Kidston, Madonna, Theresa May, Deborah Meaden, Barack Obama, Levi Roots, Oprah Winfrey

Major societal and cultural influences

The Cold War, the sexual revolution, civil rights, flower power, legalisation of homosexuality, full employment, increasing prosperity, free university education, three-day week, first moon landing, Bob Dylan, the Beatles, Led Zeppelin, *The Godfather*, *Monty Python*

Technology innovations

Colour TVs, stereo systems, tape decks, washing machines, electric kettles

Characteristics

Team-orientated, optimistic, formal, strong work ethic, used to hierarchical work structures, emotional wisdom, good networking and customer-handling skills

What does a Baby Boomer look like at work?

For a start, they will be in the office more often than their younger counterparts, because working from home is something of a modern construct. Some older managers I know can still be deeply suspicious of staff wanting to work remotely, because of an assumption that they're having a duvet day. Boomers were brought up in an environment when nine to five (at least) was the norm, you left work for the day and that was it, and no one ever contacted you at weekends or on holiday unless it was an emergency.

They will even be there when they're poorly: Boomers tend not to go off sick – even when they should – driven by their strong work ethic and their expectations of what is acceptable in the workplace. Contrast that with younger people, who will often ask in an interview how many days' sick leave they would be allowed each year. If you want a diverse workforce that isn't regularly decimated by the latest bug, you've got to be prepared to say to an older worker: 'Look, please don't come in with the flu.'

Baby Boomers will also stay in their jobs for longer, assuming there is a steady career path to follow. They think that too many changes on your CV is a bad thing. They are acclimatised to a business environment where whole careers were spent working up to an office of one's own... and then a larger corner office. Status can really matter – especially if it comes with a job title that incorporates the word 'senior'.

When this generation started work, they looked enviously up the career ladder. Each rung came with a slightly higher-spec company car and a higher pay grade. Status was transparent and striven for. The typing was done by secretaries, who also ran the office diaries. That can pose something of a challenge when you explain that the company will now have a flat structure, that no one has their own office apart from a handful of managers – and even they have to clear their desks when they're away, because their offices double up as meeting rooms.

Don't believe all you read about Baby Boomers being tech-averse: remember that their contemporaries include Tim Cook and Tim Berners-Lee. But don't assume the same seamless connectivity with the rest of the world that younger people enjoy with their devices and apps.

Finally, like the younger Generation X, Boomers are happy to work on their own: set them a task and you will need to worry far less about regular monitoring and handholding than with their younger counterparts.

Generation X: 1965–1980

Famous people from Generation X

Damon Albarn, Karren Brady, Benedict Cumberbatch, Sajid Javid, Angelina Jolie, Peter Jones, Martha Lane Fox, Martin Lewis, Kylie Minogue, Elon Musk, Michelle Obama, Jamie Oliver, JK Rowling, Zadie Smith

Major societal and cultural influences

Fall of the Berlin Wall, Gulf War, AIDS, miners' strikes, shoulder pads, raves, Brixton riots, MTV, punk rock,

Michael Jackson, Thatcher, Loadsamoney, *The A-Team, Back to the Future, Knight Rider, Rainbow, Sesame Street, The Terminator*

Technology innovations

Video cameras, CDs, mobile phones, Walkman, dishwashers, Sinclair C5, first Apple Mac computers

Characteristics

Self-reliant, ambitious, hardworking, cynical, informal, resourceful

What does a Gen X look like at work?

Generation X workers are much more likely to have gone to university than Boomers – overall participation in higher education increased from 8.4% in 1970, to 19.3% in 1990 and to 33% in 2000 (Parliament UK, 2012). As such, they will have more qualifications and place a higher value on workplace training. They are hardworking – having seen through at least one recession – and keen to get on in their careers (Dearing, 1997).

They put great value on independence (Kooij et al., 2010) and tend to be more comfortable with technology such as smartphones, laptops and tablets. Set them a task, and they're content to plug away until it's completed and then deliver it back – probably having gone further than the brief because they've taken the initiative. Your appreciation and recognition matters, but you don't need to go over the top.

Depending on the sector (financial services is the exception that proves the rule), there will be more women in senior roles from Gen X than from previous generations. This is partly because attitudes towards women in the workplace have changed over recent decades and partly because there are more female graduates.

There will also be more people from ethnic minorities in Generation X than in the Boomer generation, as immigration numbers rose significantly during the sixties and seventies. Gen X staff will also be keen to advance in their careers and, while less transient than succeeding cohorts, they will be far more willing to change jobs to achieve that than Boomers were.

Although people in Generation X were born into an analogue world, they have seen plenty of changes, as well as steadily relaxing social attitudes, along the way. That means they are more tolerant of changing work practices, and they are less formal at work. Gen X will also act as a bridge between the Boomer and Millennial generations: from a period when hierarchy was cemented at the workplace to one where it is much more fluid.

Perspectives

JOHN HAMILTON-HUNT, CEO

Punter Southall Financial Management (Independent Financial Adviser)

We're a company with just shy of eighty personnel across five locations, and the age range goes from people we've just recruited straight out of university up to people in their mid-sixties... and everything in between.

Making the most of these different generations means recognising their skills and what motivates them... and, I suppose inevitably, we do have some generational friction.

With the older cohort it can be teaching old dogs new tricks: while it's certainly not true of everyone, there are some who really don't like the new technology we've introduced and who don't appreciate change either. They've done a perfectly good job the same way for decades, think they know best, and believe that's how it should work for ever and a day.

A while back we introduced some new back-office technology, and one individual simply refused to accept it – despite encouragement and training. That caused a lot of frustration from the younger guy, who was putting a lot of time and effort into helping him but getting nowhere... and couldn't understand that response.

Some in sight of retirement will not look to change if they feel they don't have to – and yes, that can be a problem for us. Perhaps we're sometimes guilty of making the glide path to retirement slightly too comfortable.

Our clients prefer to be looked after by advisers who are within ten years of their own age, and we have clients ranging from people just starting out in life to those in retirement and looking to cascade their wealth down to the next generation. Our business is based on relationships, and because Fujitsu targeted talented people from a wide array of backgrounds, to include poets, musicians and architects (DiversityQ, 2018).

Then look closely at your recruitment process. State explicitly that you welcome applications from all age brackets. Consider making additional training available to get the right candidate up to speed with current practices. This might involve basic social media marketing or building your new recruit's computer skills, for example. Instead of viewing employment breaks with suspicion, see them as a means of accumulating alternative experience and wisdom. And rethink outdated, age-related stereotypes that might blind you to the right candidate.

For example, many companies might assume that Brandon, who is age fifty-seven, is going to require a higher starting salary than John, who is fresh out of university. But Brandon is struggling to balance a full-time workload and care for his ageing parents. He would be happy to accept a part-time, lower-paid role with fewer hours and less stress. That means he may well be an excellent, affordable hire.

Meanwhile, you might think that Lisa, at age forty-eight, isn't the best fit with your company because she performed poorly in her interview compared with a recent graduate. But Lisa has not interviewed for a job in nearly fifteen years because she has been running a small business from home. Running a business has given her many valuable skills, but she may not come across as well as the graduate who has had interview training.

Recognising and eliminating this unconscious bias is key to ensuring every single position is filled with the best possible candidate – no matter what their age or their back story.

Challenges of an age-diverse workforce

The research mentioned earlier (CIPD, 2014) also delved into the potential downsides associated with managing an age-diverse workforce. The people in the front line of sorting out the challenges are HR professionals – and 17% of them in the survey ticked 'no particular challenges'. Ask employees the same question, and a third (31%) agreed. But that doesn't mean to say that there aren't any problems to be resolved. Challenges ranked highest by HR professionals include concerns around:

- Internal progression and succession planning problems (16%)

- Age stereotyping (16%)

- A lack of shared values (15%) between colleagues of different ages

When asked to tick all that apply, employees also identified the challenge of a lack of shared interests (32%), (CIPD, 2014).

That reinforces the research carried out by Backes-Gellner and Veen (2013), which identified that an age-diverse workforce may experience increasing communication or social integration problems. Schloegel et al. (2018) also concluded that age diversity creates difficulties in communication, cooperation and coordination, stating that managers need to understand differing values and social behaviours. Williams (2015) went further, proposing that managers should realise that team-building is about not only helping to forge stronger bonds between diverse age groups, but also enabling everyone to build relationships in a more complex social environment.

Challenging the stereotypes

Age stereotyping was ranked one of the top issues raised in that CIPD poll from 2014 – and not without reason, as it can lead to communication and integration issues that are also causes for concern.

In recent decades, the UK has gone *some* way to address the bias (unconscious or otherwise) against women, ethnic minorities and other minority groups, such as LGBTQ. Things have certainly improved: you only need to watch an episode of the series *Life on Mars* to see how far we have come since the early seventies! But there is another bias that still dogs society, the media and the workplace: the stereotyping of people by their age. And no, it's not a one-way street: there are plenty of lazy, inaccurate generalisations made about younger people too.

While direct discriminatory practices are easily identified and called out, the more subtle, indirect influences still need to be addressed. Posthuma and Campion (2009) and Armstrong-Stassen and Schlosser (2008) identified that older employees were regularly viewed as being less productive than younger employees, lacking intuition and not being interested in continued learning and development. 'Viewed' being the operative word. And these views could easily affect how employees and managers behave towards older workers.

This threat of stereotyping people by their age is having a real impact on older employees, who are aware of the historical discrimination. It is also exaggerated because of the cultural differences between older generations and younger ones, who are more comfortable with the speed of development as a result of the current digital revolution.

In a neat demonstration of how assumptions can be self-fulfilling, Hess et al. (2003) identified that older employees who felt more threatened by age stereotyping performed worse in cognitive tests that those who did not. In other words, if you make a person feel inadequate, they will become so.

Rating your success

There's a great deal of work to do to address issues in the workplace that are holding some businesses back. This work needs to focus on recruiting and retaining people based on their ability and capabilities, not their age.

The next chapter looks at how businesses go about doing that. But first, ask yourself some questions that should tell you how successfully you are managing an age-diverse workforce. In her excellent book *Clash of the Generations: Managing the new workplace reality*, US writer Valerie Grubb (2017) neatly sets out the key questions that every business needs to consider in order to put in place a structure that will continue to grow and prosper over the coming five to ten years.

In summary, she suggests you look at:

- Your organisation's current leadership capabilities – and whether your current employees are developing the skills to provide seamless succession planning

- Whether or not you will suffer a skills deficit because of expected retirements

- Whether or not you promote co-working and are 'age-blind' in how you value staff

- How you will sustain innovation as the workforce changes

- And, as a consequence of answering these questions, what changes you will need to make

If you haven't already asked yourself those questions, then it's time to do so. In the next few chapters, we'll look at how to move forward.

KEY POINTS

1. A six-year study by the Centre for Ageing Better (2018) found that 'when teams mix older and younger workers, productivity goes up and complex problems find more novel solutions because the strengths and weaknesses of both groups are balanced'.

2. Employees in a CIPD survey identified the benefits of an age-diverse workforce as having different perspectives, knowledge-sharing, new ideas and improved problem-solving. Additionally, one in five respondents pointed to the benefits of more innovation and better customer service (CIPD, 2014).

3. Among the many myths around older workers is that they are more likely to need time off because of poor health, but only a quarter of over-fifties took time off in 2014, compared with just under half of those aged between twenty and thirty.

4. Workers who are older than fifty are five times less likely to change jobs than those in the 20–24 age group, so employing them reduces recruitment and training costs.

5. New research among Nobel laureates suggests that older people are as creative as younger ones – but that their creativity is based on experience rather than being conceptual.

THREE
The Digital Generations

The separation of age groups into definable 'cohorts'
– each with their own approach to life and work –
might seem like an over-generalisation. After all, we
are all individuals. However, if you consider how
the political, cultural and economic landscapes have
shifted over the last fifty or sixty years, perhaps it's
no surprise that someone from a 'digital' generation
has been shaped by very different influences than an
older counterpart who was brought up in an 'analogue world'.

Characterising the Digital generations

Millennials (Generation Y), 1981–1997

Famous Millennials

Beyoncé, Justin Bieber, Lady Gaga, Keira Knightley, Alexandria Ocasio-Cortez, Daniel Radcliffe, Eddie Redmayne, Cristiano Ronaldo, Ed Sheeran, Ivanka Trump, Phoebe Waller-Bridge, Emma Watson, Prince William, Mark Zuckerberg

Major societal and cultural influences

9/11, rise of religious tensions, austerity, student debt, cyber bullying, diversity in the workplace, normalisation of LGBTQ, gig economy, veganism, celebrity blogging/vlogging, selfies, rap, grunge, 15 minutes of fame, Banksy, Kate Moss, Spice Girls, Tarantino, *Big Brother*

Technology innovations

Tamagotchi, iPods, online shopping, email, social media, smartphones, Wi-Fi, WhatsApp, Pinterest, Netflix, FitBits, videogames

Characteristics

Feedback-orientated, community-orientated, realistic, flexible, multi-tasking

What does a Millennial look like at work?

That depends on what time you look. For a start, Millennials are less likely to be at work at either end of the day, as they find it far harder to keep to a conventional 'nine to five' than older generations do. And they'll be keen to work from home when they can, and even take unpaid time off.

Millennials are also less likely to be sitting at a desk than their older colleagues. They value collaboration and co-operative working, and they look to bounce ideas off each other – regularly meeting up in different combinations, formally or informally. To connect, commune and let the creative juices flow, they need what is quaintly termed 'huddle space': cubicles, meeting rooms, coffee shops or even a bench under a tree.

Tie a Millennial to their desk and you're not likely to get the best out of them, which is where tensions with older workers can arise. Yes, they may well find it hard to come in on time, but they'll be up late at night sending you emails on something they've thought about. On the other hand, Millennials are keen to have schedules, targets and objectives mapped out for them – many of them had parents who structured their out-of-school time for them.

Millennials will be regularly checking their emails, messages and social media accounts – possibly while they're talking to you... and when they're on their own they'll probably be wearing headphones. For these digital natives, the line between their personal and work life is blurry: they often value both equally. And the technology they have grown up with allows them to move between the two relatively easily. This means that they often take their work home, but the corollary is that they also bring their personal lives into work – to an extent that would have been unimaginable for previous generations.

My Analogue peers tend to shake off their personal life when they enter the office. We tend to dress differently at work than we do at home. And while we might display a family picture discreetly on our desk, we usually won't share anything too private with colleagues unless we know them well. When we feel the need to make small talk, it's invariably on fairly light, impersonal subjects: which box set we're glued to or the fate of our team at the weekend. Your best and brightest young Digital employees, on the other hand, will come in dressed pretty much how they might go to a café with friends, and will happily share details about their dating life. And why not? It's all over their social media accounts anyway.

Call them into a team meeting to discuss the company's future trajectory and they will want to know about its purpose and social mission, what it's doing to make a positive difference. That might set off some eyebrow-raising among the (more cynical, world-weary) Analogues in the room. But that's not the biggest difference between the two generations. Millennials (and their younger counterparts, Generation Z) have sometimes, perhaps unkindly, been named the 'trophy generation' – receiving a prize not for winning but just for taking part.

When you hire Millennials, they want love from Day 1, reassurance that they're on the right track and doing all the things they need to do to take the next step up. If you don't offer that level of input, they'll be gone in a month because they'll think you don't care – and because jobs are easy to find for talented young people.

Generation Z: 1998–present

Some famous people from Generation Z

Trent Alexander-Arnold, Brooklyn Beckham, members of NCT Dream, Parkland students (David Hogg, Emma Gonzalez), Marcus Rashford, Steven Sessegnon, Greta Thunberg, Malala Yousafzai

Some major societal and cultural influences

Global terrorism, rise of populism, concern about climate change, snowflakes, mental-health awareness, sobriety, plastic pollution, gender fluidity, streaming, social media, Kardashians, *Britain's Got Talent*

Technology innovations

On-demand television, Spotify, Netflix, Google Maps, electric and hybrid cars, iPhones, iPads, camera phones, WhatsApp, cashless payments, Kindle, Xbox

Characteristics

Globally-orientated, ethnically diverse, extremely tech-savvy, socially progressive, environmentally aware. Value flexibility, a good relationship with their manager and enjoyable work (Smith & Galbraith, 2012)

What does a Gen Z look like at work?

In fairness, with the oldest Gen Zs just coming out of university, these are still early days to assess just how the youngest generation will fare at work. It is safe to say that the trends introduced by Millennials will continue – and any business now recruiting Gen Zs will have to bridge an even bigger gap between their oldest and youngest team members.

People in this generation truly are digital natives – they were probably given a smartphone before the age of ten and, before that, they'd have been practising on their older siblings' and parents' devices. For them, the world is truly at their fingertips: they think nothing of carrying on conversations (albeit in a language that older people may not fully understand) while messaging, scrolling through their social media and watching a YouTube video by the hottest new vlogger.

Their world is totally interconnected. And if employers are to reach out to young customers and clients, as well as harnessing the skills of the digital native generation, they will need to integrate Gen Zs as they are leaving university and looking to start their careers.

Here, drawn from my own experience, is one of the challenges you're going to have to deal with. It's a direct result of the lack of boundaries between their personal and working lives:

CASE STUDY: BLURRED BOUNDARIES

Not long ago, my teenage son got a job on the front desk in a sports centre. One day, his mates turned up to play football in the sports hall. Since it was quiet, and he could see the front desk from the sports hall, he thought there was no harm in joining in.

Unfortunately, the game was captured on CCTV, and his boss decided that he did not want to pay someone £10 an hour to kick a ball around. He was unceremoniously fired: a turn of events my son still cannot understand.

He remains certain that he did nothing wrong, and that this was a gross injustice.

As an employer, my sympathies are entirely with his boss. And yours are too, probably. But if you employ people in Generation Z, it is worth delving into my son's mindset. This story illustrates a key trait of younger workers, which can cause friction in the workplace if it is not carefully managed. They can't see the problem of playing football while they're meant to be working, because their personal and professional lives are so integrated. But it can lead to clashes with older workers who did not grow up in a digital environment, and who consider this behaviour inappropriate and fundamentally unserious.

Sometimes, the behaviour of the Digital generation can disturb the Analogue generation. That's why you might have to set some ground rules. You have to make sure that your office environment works for everyone.

Perspectives

TONY STILES, CREATIVE DIRECTOR

Future Kings (creative agency)

I'm one of the founders of a creative agency with offices in Bristol, Manchester and London. As you might expect, we have mostly younger people working with us... but the management team are older, and while that throws up some differences from time to time, we really do need team members of all ages.

I suppose the older generations tend to work longer hours – probably more of a habit, almost as if that's the behaviour that's expected when you go to work. That isn't to say that the younger generations don't treat work seriously – they really do – but perhaps not with such intensity. And that's not a criticism; they have more of a balanced life. Work is part of their life, while older people have more separation between the two.

I'd say they work closely together – and productively. Mentoring is part of what we do every day. Every younger team member has an older leader, so relationships are happening every day. And both learn from each other – it's a two-way street.

Younger people have a brilliant way of multi-tasking. It used to bug me to see them on social media while they work, but it doesn't seem to affect their performance; rather, it seems to act as a 'refresh' every so often. The older generation needs to learn that within reason, it's OK.

I would also say our younger team are more instinctively entrepreneurial. They're the 'slashee' generation, where they will describe themselves as a dog walker/yoga instructor/bartender: my team feel like they have the spirit to do anything. For older people, the traditional employer/employee relationship is more the norm.

We need younger generations in the creative industry: people to see things from a different viewpoint. They have new ideas which are not bound by what they think has worked or not worked before, and they are also more naturally aware of the multiple channels now available and the different ways to communicate through each of them.

But the best output is when you blend experience with that creativity and inexperience, and my older members tend to bring that strategic element.

Sometimes you need fresh ideas, at others you need to know how to get to a solution quickly. It's an alliance of the two: creativity and rationale. That isn't to say older team members can't be creative; they really can, but this is where the younger ones really play their part.

ROSA ROLO, COMMERCIAL DIRECTOR

Major Players (recruitment agency)

We have been a leading marketing and creative recruitment agency for over twenty-five years, but the last five years have seen rapid growth and we're now 105 strong and expanding by about 20% a year. That makes for an interesting challenge: how to attract diverse talents and fit them into a structure that's growing quite quickly.

Our demographics are unusual: while we have people from age nineteen up to their late fifties, with 10%

aged over fifty and another 10% over forty, our board is very young: our MD is thirty-four and the average age in our business is around thirty – so we have people managing some people who are older than them.

It's all worked incredibly well – staff who have developed into management roles in the company have the respect of the others, and everybody recognises that they're the right people to be doing those jobs. I don't see any tensions around younger people managing older people – there's just a different style of working and you need to be aware of that.

I would say that our older personnel are happiest when there are clear boundaries – being told the parameters and expectations of the job and then going off to do it. They like to know where their role stops and starts within the hierarchy. In some ways, it's easier to manage them because they take directions and instructions more readily. There's a sense of order in it. Most Millennials want a sense of purpose – why are they doing it? How does that add value to them? So it's more about coaching than giving direct instructions – getting them to think 'What's the next step?' rather than simply saying, 'This is what you're going to do.'

Generational differences

People coming into the company at the younger end are definitely different from our older staff. I'm an older Millennial and there's a sense with people of my age group that you work hard, climb up the ladder and get promoted every eighteen months (which is still a step change from my older peers). Younger ones coming through don't have that same ladder in their minds: there is this instant gratification – getting something for something the whole time. That's incredibly difficult when you're running a sales business, and you have to think more creatively about how you engage them. All the time, you're having to think about the next thing that's going to motivate them: a constant stream of targets and rewards. Having said that, if they understand the reason behind it and that reason resonates with them then they will do it regardless. However, this involves much more coaching.

I graduated in 2008, and when I was at university there was definitely the thinking that you've got to work hard, but you can do anything you want. But then we graduated into a recession. Austerity has shaped my generation – coming out and having to graft with a big student debt and finding it hard to get on the housing ladder. The perception among younger people now is that, yes, they can achieve anything they want... and do it easily. But there are other differences too.

My little sister is four years younger than me. She left university with so much debt that she never believes she's going to pay it back, or will ever own a property. She's already disenfranchised from the world of work, and life is more hand to mouth. She's not looking to get into a long-term career and buy a house.

There is also a huge freelance market now – people moving from gig to gig – so younger people have less commitment to their employers and don't stay as long. I've been in recruitment for ten years and the advice we give has changed. Then, we were advising people to stay in a job for at least two years or it would look bad on their CV. While older Millennials will still stay for two or three years on average, the average tenure of a younger Millennial is just twelve to eighteen months – and it's at the shorter end of that spectrum for the first four or five years.

I suppose it's a sense of entitlement. Social media has played a big part in that – showing lives that are unattainable leads to a belief that 'of course I'll get a good job'.

Managing expectations

Managing expectations is really challenging, not least because younger Millennials expect regular promotions – if they don't get them, they're off. So we've got lots of levels and lots of job-title changes. They also want regular one-to-ones; we need to make sure they're enjoying their surroundings, that they have continuous learning and that they are pushing themselves.

How do you retain the best people? Understand them as individuals. Spend a lot of time giving one-to-one support. Sit down with them more frequently.

We've always done monthly reviews, constantly providing positive criticism: 'This is what you've achieved this month. This is what you're working towards.' About three years ago we introduced weekly catch-ups, as we realised that a month was too long. You can find out about things and fix them quickly – and that benefits the business. Every person gets fifteen to thirty minutes from their line manager: 'How are you? How are you getting on? What do you need?'

We've also introduced six-monthly reviews, as we were growing quickly and realised that we didn't know our staff, and there was a danger that we'd make them feel like cogs in a machine. These sessions are for understanding what they want personally – and all sorts of things have come out of the woodwork. Some want to work more flexibly, others to take time out to pursue other activities... and we've been able to adjust our benefits packages.

Benefits and retaining talent

Flexible working is an important factor – originally it was more about looking after children, but increasingly it's about achieving a work-life balance. Our senior staff can work from home two days a month, and all staff can adjust their start and finish times. That suits the early risers and those who want to go out early in the evenings, as well as helping our Millennial crowd who go 'out out' to gigs, pubs and restaurants on a Tuesday night.

We advise clients that if they aren't flexible, they won't attract or keep staff. I believe 80% of Millennials think more about their package than their salary, and we advise clients on the 'soft' things that matter to younger people; companies are busy worrying about the things they regard as 'hard costs' and less on the soft benefits that would engage staff.

Older personnel will worry about their pensions, life insurance and health benefits. Younger staff want all that plus flexible working, gym membership and so on, so it's a matter of coming up with a wider set of benefits that will appeal. Sometimes I roll my eyes at another benefit being proposed, because I come from a generation where we think you should be grateful just to be working – so it can be challenging for our clients too. There can be resistance. The creative sector should be ahead of the curve on what younger people want, but ironically it's not always the case.

KEY POINTS

1. Millennials (and even more so Gen Z) need regular feedback and reassurance from their managers.
2. They are also community-oriented, adaptable, open to change, less worried about long term job security and able to multi-task.
3. Millennials and Generation Z value online and face-to-face collaboration to share ideas and let their creative juices flow, office design needs to

accommodate these informal gatherings without disturbing other workers.

4. Both Millennials and Generation Z can sometimes have work ethics that rub up against older managers – for instance expecting a higher level of flexibility to achieve a better work/life balance. However, the lines between their working and personal lives are far more blurred and they will regularly take their work home with them.

5. Many younger workers seek to find social purpose in what they do at work – and expect their employers to respond positively to their corporate responsibilities.

PART TWO

MANAGE THE GAP

FOUR

THE BUSINESS BENEFITS OF AGE DIVERSITY

The business case for age diversity

As a longstanding season ticket holder at Fulham FC, I've seen a lot of great sides over the years. Sadly, most of them went away from Craven Cottage with three points. But that's another story. The point that any football fan will appreciate is that a manager never puts their eleven best players on the pitch. That's because five of those best players might be strikers, wingers or goalkeepers. Instead, the manager puts out the team that – between them – have the mix of skills to achieve the best result. It's not just a team of eleven players, but eleven team players. And there's a big difference between the two.

Speaking from personal experience in mountaineering in the Himalayas, I've seen first-hand how the only way to get a group up (and down) a mountain safely is to select everyone for their role and have them focus on what they do best. That team could include the motivational leader who instinctively knows how to get each individual to keep going at difficult times, the orienteer who is skilled with map and compass, the person whose rope expertise you can truly count on when you hit a crevasse, the medic in the party... right down to the cooks and humble (but essential) porters.

Teams in the workplace are no different. You need a blend of abilities to succeed. And if you want your business to have that range of skills, age diversity is a strength, not a weakness. Younger members of the team might have the edge with the latest technology. They may be more open to new ideas and new ways of doing things. They may even bring more energy and enthusiasm. But older heads bring something too: soft skills that have been honed for years. They may bring leadership skills, a keen awareness of what will (or won't) work built on experience and 'hard knocks', strategic thinking, sector knowledge, emotional intelligence and customer-handling nous. These qualities will always be in demand, especially in a business world where advancing technology makes things happen faster and more efficiently, but where success will always depend on human understanding and personal chemistry.

While recruiting people of all ages is important, in the longer term it's also essential to manage the people you do have as they go up (or down) the gears of their career. Sometimes this can mean them taking a step sideways – or even down – to accommodate their changing needs and circumstances. And here's an added bonus: as your client base ages along with the rest of the population, having an age-diverse team is the way to match the profile of your customers and improve your services.

Getting the blend right

A fusion of different ways of thinking and varying life experiences enriches the workplace. That's been borne out by countless surveys and endorsements – just some of which are quoted on these pages.

In 2014, the CIPD published *Managing an Age-Diverse Workforce: Employer and Employee Views*. This reported the results of a survey that asked respondents to rank the benefits of working with colleagues of different ages in order of importance. Top of the list? Knowledge-sharing: 55% of HR professionals ranked it as the most important benefit of working with colleagues of different ages. One in five (20%) pointed to the benefits of greater innovation and enhanced customer service delivery; it was followed by enhanced customer service (14%), improved problem-solving (9%) and greater innovation (7%).

A six-year research programme involving almost 9,000 employees conducted by Wegge et al. (2012) concluded:

> When teams mix older and younger work-
> ers, productivity goes up and complex prob-
> lems find more novel solutions because the
> strengths and weaknesses of both groups are
> balanced.

There's also plenty of evidence that age-diverse work-forces are actually more creative. Backes-Gellner and Veen (2013) reviewed the data from 1,800 companies and found that 'age diversity has a positive effect on company productivity if the company engages in cre-ative rather than routine tasks'.

Older workers are an important part of this: apart from the other attributes they bring to the workplace, they can also make it a more stable environment: workers who are over fifty are five times less likely to change jobs than those in the 20–24 age group. As well as add-ing to stability, this reduces ongoing recruitment and training costs. Don't believe the myth that older work-ers are more likely to take sick leave: according to the insurance firm RIAS (BITC, 2019b), only a quarter of people over fifty took time off in 2014 due to ill-health, compared with just under half of those aged between twenty and thirty.

Employing people from different ends of the age spec-trum can be critical whatever sector you're in. And while there's a widely held assumption that young people bring creativity and older people experience, it's more nuanced than that. New research from The Ohio State University (Grabmeler, 2019), based on a study of Nobel laureates in economics, suggests that there are two cycles of creativity: one that some demonstrate early in their career (conceptual) and another that occurs later in life (experimental).

The study found evidence that the most conceptual laureate delivered their single best work at age twenty-five, while for the most experimental laureate this happened in their mid-fifties. While conceptual innovators tend to challenge conventional wisdom and come up with new ideas suddenly, experimental innovators acquire knowledge throughout their careers and then analyse, interpret and synthesise that data into new ways of understanding.

Bruce Weinberg, lead author of the study and professor of economics, said:

> Many people believe that creativity is exclusively associated with youth, but it really depends on what kind of creativity you're talking about.

Wisdom, meanwhile, is traditionally held to be the valued attribute that older generations can bring to the workplace. This comes down to the concept that there are two types of intelligence: fluid and crystallised. This theory was first proposed by English psychologist Raymond Cattell and developed with John Horn (Horn, 1965). Their take was that fluid intelligence refers to one's ability to reason and think flexibly, while crystallised intelligence is the accumulation of knowledge, facts and skills that are acquired throughout life (otherwise defined as wisdom). Fluid intelligence begins to decline after adolescence, but crystallised intelligence continues to increase throughout adulthood.

Any good manager would want to have both types of intelligence operating in their business, as well as both types of creativity.

Recruiting the best players for *your* team

Back to my sporting analogy at the top of this chapter. Twice a year in the footballing calendar there are 'transfer windows' when managers (and the people with the purse strings) go out into the marketplace and recruit new players to strengthen their squads. Getting the right players can be a fraught (and expensive) affair. There's always a huge debate in the papers and between fans about which teams have bought cannily, and which have overpaid for a player of hyped expectations but unproven ability.

The clubs deemed to have invested their money wisely are often those who have done the extra research and looked beyond the most obvious (and priciest) players. They pluck out hidden gems who might have been plying their trade at a lower level, in a struggling team or in an obscure foreign league.

How might this analogy play out in business recruitment?

CASE STUDY: THE SPECTATOR

Every year, *Spectator* magazine takes on an intern using a rather surprising process. It forbids candidates from submitting their CV. Instead, the editorial department selects its interns based on the results of an aptitude test that purposely does *not* include names, ages, qualifications or experience. Each candidate is judged on their talent alone.

This has led to some hires that some people would find surprising, including a forty-eight-year-old with no previous journalism experience, and a long-time teacher who had decided to change profession.

There is a lesson here for every company, yours included. You need to look closely at your recruitment processes to make sure that you are not overlooking unconventional – but otherwise good – candidates for the job based on assumptions about their age or previous experience. In particular, you need to make sure that you are not inadvertently turning away older workers, who perhaps may be switching careers, returning from a long break, re-entering the work-force after running their own businesses, or trying to get a full-time job after working part time.

The person you think would be too old or stuck in their ways to cope with a bustling workplace stuffed with younger people and lots of whizzy tech might – just might – be the very person you need. Not just because (with a little training or acclimatising) they can do the same things as well as everyone else in the office, but because they can bring something else to the party.

Ask almost every 'older person' who has tried to get back into work and they will tell you of multiple rejections even before getting an interview – but I could easily have made the case for turning someone away because they are 'too young'. Age is a factor in what someone can bring to their work, but it's not the only factor – or even the defining one. To maximise your talent pool, you need to give every candidate a fair shot when you recruit, irrespective of age. If you're hesitating to appoint someone who is much older (or younger) than the rest of the team because of potential conflicts, the chapters that follow will provide some ideas on how to help everyone gel.

Age bias among British employers

Workers in Britain now have protection against age discrimination. How then do older employees themselves view the way they are managed in the workplace?

The findings from a YouGov poll on age discrimination in the workplace, commissioned by the Centre for Ageing Better (2018), revealed that two-fifths of more than 1,100 employees over the age of 50 think their age would put them at a disadvantage when applying for a job; and some 27% have actually been put off applying for jobs since turning fifty, believing the job description was aimed at younger candidates. An even higher number – 32% – believe that their age has led them to being turned down for a job.

Many employees feel let down by their bosses and prevailing working practices as a direct consequence of their age. A third (32%) feel they have had fewer opportunities for training and progression as they have got older; almost as many (29%) don't feel that their workplace values older workers; and 16% think they have been managed differently or unfairly compared with younger workers.

The statistics for those who feel they can't be open with their employers about their future are hardly any rosier. Less than a quarter (24%) feel they can be frank with their manager about their career plans, while only 20% would feel confident discussing their retirement plans and only 21% feel they can talk openly about adjusting their current role to new circumstances. Unsurprisingly, more than a quarter (28%) of older employees don't think their managers are good at managing mixed-age teams.

The inevitable conclusion is that a significant number of UK employers don't have policies in place that encourage older people to work for them. They may not realise it, but it's their company that is losing out.

Making recruitment a level playing field

Having an age-diverse workforce begins at the recruitment stage. And there's plenty of evidence to show that many able older workers just don't get selected for the job even though there are increasing numbers of people in their fifties, sixties and even seventies who are eager to work and are still at their peak, with decades of experience and wisdom to offer.

A recent survey (Hughes, 2018) showed that a third of today's workforce expects to still be earning a living at seventy, while the pool of younger workers is shrinking. This is a trend that employers are going to have to accommodate. But all too often, our recruitment processes are biased towards younger candidates (even if we don't realise it or mean them to be). For example, when you provide details about a job's 'attractive benefits package', is that package tailored towards a younger crowd, or is it attractive to candidates of all ages? How about the required qualifications? If you ask for the last five years' experience, will a brilliant stay-at-home parent who has been out of the workforce for the last decade feel comfortable about applying? Or a talented career switcher, who might have all the right skills but no direct experience? All too often, older candidates feel they are not wanted and will not be taken seriously as applicants. We do not do enough to disabuse them.

To fix this problem, start by broadening your thinking around what really makes a good candidate. Goldman Sachs and General Motors, for example, have boosted their workforce by targeting mothers seeking to return to the job market (Forbes, 2019); Fujitsu targeted talented people from a wide array of backgrounds, to include poets, musicians and architects (DiversityQ, 2018).

Then look closely at your recruitment process. State explicitly that you welcome applications from all age brackets. Consider making additional training available to get the right candidate up to speed with current practices. This might involve basic social media marketing or building your new recruit's computer skills, for example. Instead of viewing employment breaks with suspicion, see them as a means of accumulating alternative experience and wisdom. And rethink outdated, age-related stereotypes that might blind you to the right candidate.

For example, many companies might assume that Brandon, who is age fifty-seven, is going to require a higher starting salary than John, who is fresh out of university. But Brandon is struggling to balance a full-time workload and care for his ageing parents. He would be happy to accept a part-time, lower-paid role with fewer hours and less stress. That means he may well be an excellent, affordable hire.

Meanwhile, you might think that Lisa, at age forty-eight, isn't the best fit with your company because she performed poorly in her interview compared with a recent graduate. But Lisa has not interviewed for a job in nearly fifteen years because she has been running a small business from home. Running a business has given her many valuable skills, but she may not come across as well as the graduate who has had interview training.

Recognising and eliminating this unconscious bias is key to ensuring every single position is filled with the best possible candidate – no matter what their age or their back story.

Challenges of an age-diverse workforce

The research mentioned earlier (CIPD, 2014) also delved into the potential downsides associated with managing an age-diverse workforce. The people in the front line of sorting out the challenges are HR professionals – and 17% of them in the survey ticked 'no particular challenges'. Ask employees the same question, and a third (31%) agreed. But that doesn't mean to say that there aren't any problems to be resolved. Challenges ranked highest by HR professionals include concerns around:

- Internal progression and succession planning problems (16%)

- Age stereotyping (16%)

- A lack of shared values (15%) between colleagues of different ages

When asked to tick all that apply, employees also identified the challenge of a lack of shared interests (32%), (CIPD, 2014).

That reinforces the research carried out by Backes-Gellner and Veen (2013), which identified that an age-diverse workforce may experience increasing communication or social integration problems. Schloegel et al. (2018) also concluded that age diversity creates difficulties in communication, cooperation and coordination, stating that managers need to understand differing values and social behaviours. Williams (2015) went further, proposing that managers should realise that team-building is about not only helping to forge stronger bonds between diverse age groups, but also enabling everyone to build relationships in a more complex social environment.

Challenging the stereotypes

Age stereotyping was ranked one of the top issues raised in that CIPD poll from 2014 – and not without reason, as it can lead to communication and integration issues that are also causes for concern.

In recent decades, the UK has gone *some* way to address the bias (unconscious or otherwise) against women, ethnic minorities and other minority groups, such as LGBTQ. Things have certainly improved: you only need to watch an episode of the series *Life on Mars* to see how far we have come since the early seventies! But there is another bias that still dogs society, the media and the workplace: the stereotyping of people by their age. And no, it's not a one-way street: there are plenty of lazy, inaccurate generalisations made about younger people too.

While direct discriminatory practices are easily identified and called out, the more subtle, indirect influences still need to be addressed. Posthuma and Campion (2009) and Armstrong-Stassen and Schlosser (2008) identified that older employees were regularly viewed as being less productive than younger employees, lacking intuition and not being interested in continued learning and development. 'Viewed' being the operative word. And these views could easily affect how employees and managers behave towards older workers.

This threat of stereotyping people by their age is having a real impact on older employees, who are aware of the historical discrimination. It is also exaggerated because of the cultural differences between older generations and younger ones, who are more comfortable with the speed of development as a result of the current digital revolution.

In a neat demonstration of how assumptions can be self-fulfilling, Hess et al. (2003) identified that older employees who felt more threatened by age stereotyping performed worse in cognitive tests that those who did not. In other words, if you make a person feel inadequate, they will become so.

Rating your success

There's a great deal of work to do to address issues in the workplace that are holding some businesses back. This work needs to focus on recruiting and retaining people based on their ability and capabilities, not their age.

The next chapter looks at how businesses go about doing that. But first, ask yourself some questions that should tell you how successfully you are managing an age-diverse workforce. In her excellent book *Clash of the Generations: Managing the new workplace reality*, US writer Valerie Grubb (2017) neatly sets out the key questions that every business needs to consider in order to put in place a structure that will continue to grow and prosper over the coming five to ten years.

In summary, she suggests you look at:

- Your organisation's current leadership capabilities – and whether your current employees are developing the skills to provide seamless succession planning

- Whether or not you will suffer a skills deficit because of expected retirements

- Whether or not you promote co-working and are 'age-blind' in how you value staff

- How you will sustain innovation as the workforce changes

- And, as a consequence of answering these questions, what changes you will need to make

If you haven't already asked yourself those questions, then it's time to do so. In the next few chapters, we'll look at how to move forward.

KEY POINTS

1. A six-year study by the Centre for Ageing Better (2018) found that 'when teams mix older and younger workers, productivity goes up and complex problems find more novel solutions

because the strengths and weaknesses of both groups are balanced'.

2. Employees in a CIPD survey identified the benefits of an age-diverse workforce as having different perspectives, knowledge-sharing, new ideas and improved problem-solving. Additionally, one in five respondents pointed to the benefits of more innovation and better customer service (CIPD, 2014).

3. Among the many myths around older workers is that they are more likely to need time off because of poor health, but only a quarter of over-fifties took time off in 2014, compared with just under half of those aged between twenty and thirty.

4. Workers who are older than fifty are five times less likely to change jobs than those in the 20–24 age group, so employing them reduces recruitment and training costs.

5. New research among Nobel laureates suggests that older people are as creative as younger ones – but that their creativity is based on experience rather than being conceptual.

FIVE

Intergenerational Management

Age diversity is a strength

My company began with a fairly conventional hierarchy of departments led by eight managers, all of whom made up the management board. But it wasn't long before I made a major shift.

Those eight managers were (on balance) older but likely to remain with the company for some time to come. As welcome as that continuity would be, it posed a problem: what would happen to all the talented younger people coming up through the ranks? How could I be sure their opinions and ideas would get through to me? How could I keep all that talent in the company when they were looking to progress?

The answer was to replace the board with seven operating committees, allowing a broader, more diverse group of individuals to become involved in the leadership and strategy of the business. Importantly, this restructure ensured fairness and diversity in the management structure and decision-making process, which helped to overcome any biases (implicit or otherwise) that may have undermined the way the previous management board made decisions. Now, in common with many companies where the work is highly project-based, I have truly intergenerational, multi-disciplinary teams – and each individual has a title specific to their role in the team.

Flexibility is built in at every level. Roles can change as projects come and go, people can switch between teams to take on new roles and build their careers, and individual salaries can go up to reflect the role a person is playing (without affecting a delicate hierarchy). Equally, employees can move sideways to a more flexible role, move to less demanding positions or even go part time if their circumstances change. It's that level of pliancy which has allowed us to grow extremely rapidly and hold on to a relatively high proportion of talented staff. And I will promote people as often as they deserve it, rather than waiting for jobs to become vacant: if more of my employees earn bigger salaries, it shows the company is doing well.

The company has also built in mechanisms to smooth teamworking and ensure that any potential intergenerational misunderstandings are flagged up quickly. Part of this process is the structure of the regular team meetings: at the start of each gathering, everyone has the chance to say how they'd score the previous month in terms of their work, wellbeing and private life. This is integral to the continuous learning process. In these 'sign-in sessions', no one is obliged to go into detail, and some simply stand up and say 'X out of ten' and sit down again. But it's surprising how many are quite happy to be frank about what's going on in their work and in their life, clearing the air before we get on to more nitty-gritty work-related issues.

For example, in one revelatory session, three of the older team members said they were having major problems trying to care for their ageing parents. This really helped younger members of the team understand the pressures their colleagues were under. On another occasion, it revealed a problem in an intergenerational working relationship:

CASE STUDY: NIPPING PROBLEMS IN THE BUD

At the start of one team meeting, a younger employee marked her last month at work very low out of ten. She didn't say why, despite the fact that she was usually quite open.

I caught up with her later and it transpired that she felt that her (older) manager never listened to her ideas and seemed intent on continuing to do things the way they had always been done. When I spoke to her manager, he hadn't recognised that as a problem: why change something that had always worked in the past? However, he did feel his younger colleague was quite challenging (read 'disrespectful'), bearing in mind his seniority.

Both of these people make really important contributions to the company. I certainly didn't want to see either of them disaffected or leave. But it was obvious that this was a classic conflict of the generations: one side questioned the 'old way' of doing things, and the other felt threatened by that. Neither side was right – or wrong.

To tackle this particular problem, I had several sessions with each of them, getting them to understand the other's perspective and make some compromises. We did get there... eventually.

In situations like this, being a manager isn't just about working out what your team members need and treating them as individuals, as critical as that is. It's also about recognising the dynamics of the relationships between different members of the team and finding ways that they can work together. That's time-consuming for management. It involves getting both parties to feel they are being listened to (and that their concerns are being acted on), and that takes mentoring at both ends of the age spectrum.

The benefits of age diversity are considerable, but they need working at. That's what the next section begins to explore.

Understanding different work ethics

You have asked one of your younger workers to deliver a key report. It lands on your desk, on time. You open it, to find... that it delivers exactly what you asked for.

Nothing more. Nothing less. It sounds acceptable, but the truth is that many managers would be disappointed. To prove their worth and excellence, goes the maxim of management, employees need to over-deliver, not just meet the brief. When your output is always the exact minimum required, you are seen as not committed, lacking initiative – and, well, lazy.

In my experience, this is a trap that often ensnares younger workers. It is one of the reasons they are widely regarded as having a poor work ethic. The reality is far more complicated – and interesting. The science supports the fact that younger workers do not want to work as hard as their predecessors. The Monitoring the Future project has surveyed 45,500 Americans students per year since 1976 – through adolescence into adulthood (Twenge, 2016). This fascinating and comprehensive study has picked up on unfolding trends and differences in attitudes on a huge range of topics among different cohorts.

One of the important conclusions is that younger generations are more likely to value leisure over working time than their older counterparts. In raw percentages, the results show that 38% of younger employees 'don't want to work hard', as opposed to 26% of Baby Boomers. Less than half are willing to work overtime, compared with 56% of people in Generation X and 59% of Baby Boomers (Twenge, 2016). These, incidentally, are *their* views – not observations made by outsiders. While this is a US study, it tallies precisely with UK studies and my experience in UK businesses.

Knowing how keen young workers are to balance their work and their personal lives is vital to anyone managing them – especially if that person is older than them and has a different outlook. Younger workers prioritise flexibility at work, so they can make and keep personal and social commitments. But this does not mean they do not work hard. It simply means that the work ethic is not as important to them as other values.

In fact, it seems to me that these digital natives, who are value-driven and routinely prioritise meaningful work over pay, care a lot about contributing and adding value. They just go about it differently. While they may not over-deliver in the traditional sense, they do so in other areas – specifically, on the process of delivering your project. They are probably spending hours doing research late at night or on weekends, because they are quite happy working outside the office and outside traditional working hours. The lines between their lives inside and outside work are blurred, quite possibly because most businesses no longer shut at 5.30pm and open again at 9am.

Here's an example from one of my businesses.

CASE STUDY: HOW DIGITAL NATIVES WORK

A young member of the tech team thought the business could be run more efficiently if there was an app for part of what we do. So, he built one – entirely in his own time. (This way of doing things is so common that there's even a name for it – it's called 'skunk work', a term which goes back to a research group working informally together during World War II). No one had asked for it, but he found the work exciting and thought the app could be useful.

I evaluated the project and encouraged this staff member to continue working on the app in business hours. Ultimately, we didn't adopt it for the business, but the employee's extra-curricular work showed us not only what he is capable of but also where the innovation comes from in many businesses nowadays.

As a manager, you can look at your younger workers and notice that they don't like doing the nine to five, or they're peeking at their social media feeds from time to time, or they're asking to buy extra holidays so they can take a four-week break. You might conclude that they're not committed to the business and not working hard enough. But they are, and they do. Their work simply looks different from what you, and many of your older workers, may be used to.

The problem is that much of the effort they make – work that supports the success of your business – is often unseen by managers and peers. It takes place outside the workplace, outside work hours, and – as is the nature of research – behind the scenes. You can imagine how frustrating this is for this cohort, whose work ethic is unfairly maligned and whose contributions are often under-appreciated. It's no good for businesses either, who are failing to recognise the value that their younger employees bring and to take advantage of what they have to offer.

That's why we need to start thinking about employees' contributions differently. Make sure that input and process – *how* your staff deliver the work – is valued across your organisation as much as outcomes are. Include this, for example, in work evaluations – not just for your younger workers but for all employees. After all, everyone will benefit from having their efforts recognised, whether they are digital natives or not.

Part of establishing a culture in the workplace that gets the best out of everyone is building a management structure that benefits people of all ages. I have mentioned the fairly flat structure in my business, with intergenerational teams. That solves several issues. One is that it allows older workers, should they wish, to take a step sideways – perhaps doing fewer hours, taking on less responsibility or assuming a different role in the organisation that recognises and makes full use of their skills (such as strategic or mentoring skills). This opens up the opportunity to discuss training for future business skills with them: something every business is going to have to deal with as the pace of technology changes, familiar roles disappear and new ones emerge. A flat structure also allows younger people (who relish having their future spelled out for them) to progress in the organisation, rather than waiting for their boss to retire.

Another way to get the best out of all employees, regardless of their age, is to put in place policies that promote health and wellbeing. Older, health-conscious Analogues will respond well to company policies that take positive steps towards a healthier working environment. Digital generations also value wellbeing and a work-life balance, and in the long term they'll be grateful for the healthcare and lifestyle benefits you offer to support an older workforce. What works well for one generation can also work well for others.

Recruitment: the first step towards a multi-generational workforce

This section is all about developing the talent in your company. Talent is your single biggest asset. But for any business, that road begins with appointing the right people.

In just a few short years, my company has been on a rapid growth curve: up from a workforce of one (me!) to around a hundred and fifty. I achieved this in three distinct ways. In the first months, I headhunted several people I trusted to accompany me on the journey: seasoned professionals who were well versed in the trials of building a new venture from scratch. Secondly, I recruited a series of people to fill key roles – junior and senior. That process is ongoing. Thirdly, the company has grown by acquiring a series of independent financial adviser (IFA) businesses.

The team I have now is hugely diverse, from recent school leavers to those who are past State Pension age – hence my interest in managing multiple generations. While managing people you've 'inherited' presents its own set of challenges (some of which I'll deal with later), fuelling growth by taking on the right people is the starting point for most enterprises. Earlier, I commended never making assumptions about the person sitting across from you in an interview just because they don't seem to fit the profile you imagined when you wrote the job spec. Being open minded on age is a big part of that – whether someone younger or older applies.

Older applicants

Older applicants can bring something to the workplace that younger cohorts may not: experience, soft skills and a strong work ethic, for example. Many older professionals out there have been 'let go' by their employers – especially in sectors such as finance and law, where the default has been to jettison personnel once they reach the age of fifty-five. Many are not too badly off because they've got a DB pension to fall back on, and they can choose whether or not to re-enter the world of work. However, a generation is starting to come through without that DB safety net – and that trend is set to continue. The golden age of company pensions is coming to an end, and the next generation will be a much poorer one. There's a good chance that many of those older workers will find it very difficult to get a decent pension together. They can't afford to be made redundant at age fifty-five.

This is a rich talent pool to fish in, but there are caveats. On more than one occasion I've interviewed an older person who assumes that because they have worked their way up to earning a certain amount, they can still command that amount, or even more. That's not how it works today, and some older applicants need to change this mindset if they are to get back into employment. I'm not paying for age; I'm paying for skills. And if the job they are going for has a set of competencies that can be fulfilled by someone who hasn't risen so far up the ranks, why would I pay beyond the market rate?

Should that be the end of the conversation with them? Not necessarily. From a company's perspective, especially those working to a budget, this is a huge opportunity to acquire a highly experienced person. If the applicant looks at their situation again and recognises that their outgoings aren't what they were and that there is no shame in recalibrating, they might well become available. Equally, if they can afford to do so, there may be an opportunity for them to work three days a week or on a contract basis – with all the work-life balance advantages that offers. Indeed, the recession has already pushed many older people into becoming contractors.

Take that idea on board when you next recruit. There's a bit of a blind spot with many businesses – an opportunity being missed: you can take talented people on part time. A good person can give you as much value in three days as a lesser one can in five.

Younger applicants

The flip side is younger applicants going for a job without having any relevant experience. For instance, you might find that someone applying for a marketing role has never worked in marketing but they have set up a successful YouTube channel or built up 100,000 followers on Instagram.

John (our Boomer-generation head of marketing) has been fantastically successful at hiring talented young Digitals who appear to be right on top of how to communicate with an audience – especially a younger one – but need support to steer their obvious talents in the right direction. And this is where older, wiser heads in the company can provide the mentoring, and garner the best of both worlds.

Managing workers who are older than you

'Can you put together a PowerPoint for our next team meeting, about last month's sales figures?'

The employee suddenly looks anxious. 'Um... Is it really necessary? Shouldn't we just do a verbal presentation? Lots of people will prefer it.'

The real reason? Your staff member, in their early sixties, has never prepared a PowerPoint before. And they have no idea where to start. When their younger manager realises what is really going on, they scoff inwardly at the older employee's lack of technical skills. They assign the PowerPoint presentation to someone else – 'Don't worry, I'll take care of it' – and mentally dismiss the older employee as a 'has-been'.

They don't understand, or don't care, that this is actually one of the most accomplished members of the team.

As the workforce ages, scenes like this threaten to become increasingly common. How are you going to manage a situation where, for a host of reasons (including older workers moving sideways or winding down), you will be managing colleagues who have different ways of working – ways that you will perceive as antiquated and not part of the modern way of doing business? Just how do you ensure that your older employees are given the support they need to thrive in the modern workplace, and that their potential to contribute is valued and recognised?

The key is to create an environment in which age diversity is genuinely respected. You need to publish policies that prevent discrimination against your older employees and nurture an environment in which different generations can work productively together. But policies, on paper, will make no difference. Not unless your team members have genuinely bought into your vision of a company where people of different ages, with their different skills, abilities and experiences, can work seamlessly together, supporting each other and drawing on each other's strengths.

The scenario of a younger manager brushing aside an older employee because they don't know their way around PowerPoint could easily happen in a company that on paper is 'committed to age diversity'. But it wouldn't happen in a company in which that was genuinely the prevailing culture.

Making that happen is a big task. But it is possible. Over the past few decades, most companies have made enormous strides with instilling a culture of gender, ethnic and cultural diversity at work. The majority of businesses have made a conscious effort to create workplaces in which women and minorities are celebrated and treated equally, and diversity is recognised as a net asset to the business. While there is still some way to go, the result is a significant cultural shift.

Age diversity is rarely championed in the same way – but it could be. Start by rolling age into your initiatives around diversity. Help your employees understand, and genuinely buy into, the fact that working in a multi-generational environment brings enormous benefits, just as working in a multi-cultural environment does.

Everyone has knowledge to share. For instance, employees in older generations have a lot of institutional and operational knowledge, which without them would be lost. You could create cross-generational mentoring programmes to share that knowledge. This means thinking about how you need to structure and change your business to bring knowledge-sharing about. With these programmes in place, when an older employee confesses that they have never used PowerPoint, the reaction is never eye-rolling and exasperation but an offer of help. Your younger employee knows that the older staff member has helped them to navigate other issues in the past, because the information flows in both directions – and they are happy to reciprocate.

That is a workplace where staff believe that age diversity has intrinsic value.

Busting some myths about older workers

Myth 1: Older workers are behind with technology

What percentage of people in their late sixties and early seventies have a social media profile? The answer, which might surprise you, has interesting implications as our workforce ages. Many people may assume that only a small minority of people in this age bracket are on social media. After all, social media is the preserve of the young(er), right?

Not so. According to the Office for National Statistics (ONS, 2018), in the last decade the 65–74 age range has seen the single largest increase in recent internet use, up from 53% in 2011 to 83% in 2019. Almost half (47%) of people over the age of seventy-five were on social media in 2019, up from a mere 20% in 2011. What this shows is that when it comes to older people, stereotypes abound. We have to examine them carefully to see whether they have any basis in reality – especially when it comes to the workplace.

You see, the law doesn't stop older people from working. But very often, stereotypes do. For example, there is a general perception that older workers can't cope with technology, or don't want to take part in technology training. Let's say that one of your managers needs to send some of your employees on an Excel training course, and, looking at the candidates, rules out employees who are over the age of sixty. The reason? 'They'll find it too hard anyway.'

Or perhaps, as in the example earlier, an employee in their sixties admits that they have never used PowerPoint. The manager tells them not to worry about it – they will ask another employee to create the slide deck, depriving the older staff member of the opportunity to present to the team.

In reality, older people are often eager to use tech, if only they are given the opportunity. People between the ages of fifty-five and sixty-four are the fastest-growing users of IT (Barrett & Bourke, 2013). They might need extra time to learn to use the tools proficiently, but this is quite different from being 'unable to cope'. Perhaps they could be assisted to learn by members of their own age group, who will understand the way they absorb information. Or they could learn through a cross-mentoring arrangement where in return for help with IT they regularly assist a younger person get to grips with aspects of the workplace that they take for granted.

Myth 2: Older workers are resistant to change

There is often a perception that older workers don't like their job descriptions to evolve, and that they don't like change in the company. This positions them as obstacles in a fast-changing business. Is this really true, though, or are older workers simply more cautious about change?

Over the years, they might have seen organisations go through evolution after evolution. Sometimes they might have witnessed change for change's sake as a new manager or business owner has come in with a point to prove. They may have been disappointed by changes in the past. They might be worried about losing control, or losing face if their new duties are less suited to their abilities. This cautiousness does not imply an inherent resistance to change. It simply indicates that older workers may need more encouragement to embrace it.

The problem with stereotypes is that they are often inaccurate – and as long as they persist, they can stop you from realising the benefits of an age-diverse team of staff, and prevent you from getting the best out of your ageing workforce.

Some people in your organisation will shy away from entrusting important tasks to older people and will fail to see the many ways that they could contribute and support younger workers. To deal with this, managers need to overcome any tendency to stereotype. The first step is simply to raise awareness with managers and employees that they may be influenced by unconscious biases around age. The more aware they are, the more they will be able to self-correct their thinking – and behaviour. Then re-enforce this with formal policies.

Make clear that in your company employees of all ages are to be treated equally, and insist on these policies being implemented. The more you do this, the easier it will be to establish a culture where younger workers think of their older peers realistically, generously and supportively.

Appreciating the contribution of younger workers

CASE STUDY: 'CAN YOU HELP ME FIX MY BIKE?'

A friend of mine had just opened the door to his flat. Before him stood a young boy, no older than twelve or thirteen years old, who lived in the flat above. The boy had punctured a tyre and his mother had sent him to the neighbour to get some help. The chap, who is in his fifties, was happy to oblige, but he later told me that he was astonished by one thing – which has important implications for every workplace.

According to my friend, the boy never actually looked at him while asking for help. He was too busy looking at his phone. And it was the same story while my friend fixed the bike. Instead of talking to him, the boy was surfing the internet and texting his friends. My friend told me how frustrated he was, initially, by the boy's rude behaviour. He was helping him, but the boy seemed oblivious and ungrateful.

But on reflection, my friend changed his mind. He came to realise that it wasn't the boy's fault. The younger generation of digital natives are almost anatomically attached to their phones in a way that is inconceivable to people who did not grow up with smartphones in their pockets. It's their primary way of communicating, and of feeling and staying connected to their wider circle.

The 'A Decade of Digital Dependency' report (Ofcom, 2018) showed that older and younger generations differ in what they see as acceptable smartphone use. For example, those in the 15–24 age bracket spend on average four hours a day using their phone (compared with two hours and forty-nine minutes for all other adults). The 15–24 age group also checked their phones every 8.6 minutes – more frequently than any other age group.

Returning to my example, it wasn't a question of manners. This generation considers it normal to communicate digitally, even when they are face to face with someone else. Listening to this story, it occurred to me that in a few years' time, these two people could one day become co-workers.

What would their encounter be like in the office? We don't have to guess, because these two generations already regularly collide, and sometimes struggle to understand each other, in the workplace. I can already see the digital native – by now in his early twenties – sitting in meetings, fiddling with his phone and texting during other people's presentations. Equally, I can visualise the older worker sitting opposite him at the table, silently fuming and condemning his young colleague for being disrespectful: 'Not a team player.'

Or take the multi-tasking younger worker sitting at her desk, simultaneously working on her computer, sending a text message and watching a movie playing in the background. The older worker who is trying, in vain, to attract her attention, gets increasingly annoyed.

In these situations, both older workers conclude that their younger colleague is distracted and cannot do the job. These kinds of clashes are only going to increase as an influx of digital natives enters the workplace, especially as the older generation will be working far longer before retiring. So how can you help these colleagues work together, respectfully and productively?

First, my generation must accept the truth articulated by my friend who fixed the boy's bike. The younger generation are not being rude, egocentric or difficult when they communicate with people on their phone, even if they are in the room – or in conversation – with someone else who is standing right in front of them. It's simply the way they are. The norms of communication have changed, and we are not going to reverse that.

But beyond that, we need to continue fostering a workplace that recognises the skills and insight each group brings to the table. The digital natives have – among other things – a deep understanding of technology and how it is used in the modern world. Those who are older have years of industry knowledge and life experience to share.

Both are valuable. Both must be equally respected. And where the generations inevitably do collide, we need to mentor and help people through those situations, so they can see each other for who they are and be generous about each other – instead of getting caught up in stereotypes and misunderstandings.

The value of wisdom

Like most business managers, I love TED talks. They frequently give you a new perspective or fresh insight that really makes you look again at how you run your company or manage the people around you.

Chip Conley's 2018 talk, 'What Baby Boomers Can Learn from Millennials at Work – and Vice Versa', is a must for anyone looking to manage an age-diverse workforce. It's only twelve minutes long, and it contains a couple of gems.

Born in 1960 and so a late Baby Boomer, Conley describes his third day working with Airbnb. He'd been taken on by what was then a relatively new company to act as a sounding board for the young 'techies' in the company.

He walked into a boardroom where he was by far the oldest person in the room, with people talking a language he could not understand. 'This,' he says, 'was not my natural habitat.'

All the other people in the room knew how the interface of Airbnb should work. He'd been brought into the business because of his success in the hospitality sector. He knew what guests expected from their stay.

However, after that initial feeling of being out of his depth, Conley realised that he could really add value to the business by mentoring the younger people there. As he points out, they also ended up mentoring him.

The talk is important viewing for anyone seeking to manage an intergenerational team – not least because Conley highlights the challenge that many owners of young businesses face: with their natural entrepreneurial flair they have spotted a gap in the market and created a start-up with a clever app or digital solution. But then they're expected to have management skills too.

This is the vital gap which an older head can fill, and where the wisdom of elders can play a critical role. As Conley says: 'We actually get smarter and wiser about our humanity as we age.'

Tapping into that well of wealth is already an opportunity for business managers. But as more Digitals enter the world of work and set up the whizzy new companies of the future, that resource will become even more important.

In Conley's words: 'I believe, looking at the modern workplace, that the trade agreement of our time is opening up these intergenerational pipelines of wisdom so that we can all learn from each other.'

KEY POINTS

1. Among younger employees, 38% say they 'don't want to work hard', as opposed to 26% of Baby Boomers. And less than half are willing to work overtime, compared with 56% of people in Generation X and 59% of Baby Boomers.

2. Digitals prioritise flexibility at work, so they can make and keep personal and social commitments. They still work hard, but the work ethic is not as important to them as other values are.

3. Ageist stereotypes abound in society. They are often inaccurate, and they can stop you from realising the benefits of an age-diverse workforce and prevent you from getting the best out of your ageing workforce.

4. To tackle inherent ageism, start by including age in any diversity initiatives you have. Help your employees understand and buy into the enormous benefits of working in a multi-generational environment.

SIX

Organisational Style And Structure

The times they are a-changin'

Born in 1970, I'm a fairly classic Analogue. I spent my teenage years rock climbing on the sea cliffs in Dorset and gritstone quarries in the Peak District, and mountaineering in the Alps as often as I could (I had climbed the Matterhorn and Mont Blanc by the time I was nineteen). However, I did not spend lots of time studying, and after some dismal A-level results I found myself looking for work. I saw an advert for an office trainee in the *Southern Evening Echo*, applied and got it.

The first eighteen months at the bottom of the pile weren't great: they included a great deal of tea making, buying cream cakes for the office secretaries and writing addresses on envelopes by hand... but I don't remember complaining. That first Christmas, as the most junior person in the office, it was expected that I'd be the one to go out into the park (in my suit) and dig some soil for the Christmas tree. Of course, I got on with it. At least, I thought, next year someone else will be junior to me.

I really can't imagine that happening now.

Back in those days, being managed by the Silent Generation or Baby Boomers, it was a 'one size fits all' approach: this is how it's always been done; this is how you have to do it now. It was a pretty rigid structure, and you achieved advancement when someone higher up than you moved up a peg... or dropped off. I can't recall anyone at my interview asking me why I wanted to work there, and I didn't ask about anything beyond the working hours and salary. I was there to earn a living and make my way up the corporate tree.

As I moved on in my career to focus on sales, management meetings revolved around targets and the occasional new product launch. Success was measured in turnover and profits. Customer satisfaction levels only mattered as a metric in so far as they affected repeat sales. My managers in my early career were very hands-off. They didn't know what was going on in my private life, or the names of my wife or children. They weren't those types of managers. Many of them, if I'm honest, were bullies.

You kept your head down and did your stint on each rung of the ladder. The business was structured so that, with time served and by displaying a certain amount of expertise you made your way to the top. That said, many were there because of the hierarchical structure of the business rather than their talent.

No doubt there are still businesses out there modelled on 'how it's always been done'. But they are a dying breed – and for a good reason. It's hard for them to attract and retain talented people. Most organisations are much flatter now – enabling talent to shine through, to the benefit of the company as much as the individual. Someone can get to an influential position in a short space of time.

I'm not like one of my old bosses, who habitually applied pretty much the same management techniques to all the staff. I have to deeply understand each individual's motivations: what drives them, what they like and dislike, how much feedback they want, how much encouragement they need, and what I need to do to keep them in the company.

Managing Millennials' mission

Managing a multi-generational workforce means that you need to appreciate the differences between them. And one of the key differences between the generations is their mission at work. Wind back thirty years:

the people in my office weren't there to change the world. If that's what they'd wanted to do, they'd have gone to work for a charity – and been paid less as a result. This is not how the Digital generations see the world of work.

Remember, the lines between the worlds of work and non-work are far more blurred for younger generations. What they believe in, and why they come to work for you – rather than for someone else – is at the heart of that. Members of my team who are in the Digital generations want to know what the company stands for and how it plans to play its part in making the world a better place. A study conducted by Pew Research Centre (2010) found that Millennials are more motivated by making a difference than by their salary, and that they want to work for organisations that focus on purpose, not just profit. Only 15% were motivated by the prospect of a high-paying career. Millennials also see making a difference as the way for a business to win and retain customers. A report by Deloitte (2017) shows that this cohort considers the top three values that support long-term business success to be treating people fairly, ethics and customer focus.

Young people want evidence of purpose and social mission from their employer. As a manager, it's no good rolling your eyes when this topic comes up, and assuming that corporate responsibilities are a fad to which you pay lip service. This is like the writing on a stick of rock: it goes right through to your customers and clients. Consumers in the Digital generation expect companies to go beyond their legal obligations and act ethically and responsibly.

Companies have long had logos, branding and strap lines, but 'social mission' is a much broader component, popularised by businesses like Google and Apple. It's a far more complicated and intrinsic message about your business's relationship with the world. Check out some of the world's biggest businesses and you'll find that, in between promises to sell great products, they weave in a 'higher purpose' that will make their customers, staff and even their shareholders feel good about them:

- **Microsoft:** 'To empower every person and every organisation on the planet to achieve more.'

- **General Motors:** 'We envision a future of zero crashes, zero emissions and zero congestion, and we have committed ourselves to leading the way toward this future.'

- **Procter & Gamble:** 'We will provide branded products and services of superior quality and value that improve the lives of the world's consumers, now and for generations to come.'

- **Unilever:** 'To supporting sustainability and providing our consumers around the world with the products they need to look good, feel good and get more out of life.'

While my generation (Generation X) in particular can be quite cynical about this sort of stuff, younger people lap it up. Their lives are far more interconnected, and they connect through shared values. That applies not just to their friendship and interest groups, but also to the company they work for and those they buy from. Their exposure to community and global issues through social media means that, beyond their desire for a work-life balance, their personal values and work ethic often align.

However, there is one caveat: companies with grand-sounding mission statements have to walk the walk: any disconnect between a business's avowed mission and their actions is rapidly spotted. Watch what happens on a company's Twitter feed when it's found to be exploiting cheap labour overseas, not looking after its customers or finding ways to avoid paying the minimum wage.

The reason Boomers and, even more so, Gen X can be quite scornful about this sort of stuff is that we've all seen brands position and constantly reposition themselves. Sometimes this seems as if they can't make up their minds what they stand for, and sometimes they say they're one thing but they turn out not to be that thing. In my business, when I ran a workshop to decide a mission to which we can align ourselves, some team members in the older generations saw it as a tick-box exercise. But managers need to adopt a strong (and credible) set of corporate values and mission if they are to retain and engage the Digital generation in the workplace.

Think of it as an extension of Maslow's hierarchy of needs (where individuals progress through a series of personal needs – from basic requirements like food, water and shelter on to love, friendship and family); because they've grown up in a more affluent world than the Analogue generations, Digitals have gone beyond meeting basic needs and are moving into the esteem and self-actualisation zones. They want a purpose in going to work. They want to think – and say to their friends – 'I'm ultimately making people's lives better, making a positive difference to the world.'

It's been well reported in recent years that volunteering levels are rising among the younger generations, but falling among the older ones. Figures released in 2017 by consultancy nfpSynergy (Kay, 2017) showed that between 2004 and 2017, the proportion of people in the 16–24 age group who volunteer rose from 15% to 29%.

Here's an example from my business.

CASE STUDY: MAKING A DIFFERENCE

My company is a retirement savings business, and its mission is to build a more financially informed and secure society. Ultimately, that's all about improving people's financial lives. By maintaining that perspective, we do a better job for our clients; and I retain and recruit good people.

But the Digitals in our office asked: 'Can't we go beyond giving employed people better pensions, health insurance and so on? Can't we improve the life of the guy living on the street over there?'

We then aligned ourselves with a not-for-profit organisation – The Money Charity. Their mission is financial education, and they improve people's lives through workshops in the community. We give our team the opportunity to volunteer on company time (at the moment, it's just three half-days a year) and they go into schools, community centres and even prisons to deliver workshops.

So far, a dozen of our staff have done this, all of whom are younger ones. Feeling that I need to walk the walk too, I'm becoming a trustee of the charity. My assistant has also arranged for volunteers to go the junior school next door to the office in Whitechapel and read to the children at lunchtimes. Again, it's the Millennials who are joining her.

Personally speaking, I've long wanted to work for an organisation with a social purpose. That's why I never felt comfortable in the larger organisation in my early career – and I'm much more comfortable now. Every company can do its 'bit', and as a manager, it's important to have this in the mix to recruit and retain Millennials – but to recognise that your older staff will be a bit more cynical, and not force them to join in. They'll come around to it at their own pace. Think about whether it's a symptom of caring less... or whether they have less available time.

Understanding a younger person's perspective

How many jobs did you have before you started full-time work?

The number you give will probably be a good guide to the generation you're in. Even among better-off families, it used to be the norm for youngsters to take on a holiday or weekend job – not just to earn some pocket money but also to learn about the world of work.

Me? I had jobs as a paperboy, a mechanics workshop skivvy, a petrol station cashier, a plumber's mate, a building labourer, a potato peeler in a chip shop, a warehouse worker and a farmhand on a clay pigeon shoot. Thanks to this experience, by the age of eighteen I had a fair idea of what to expect on my first day in a suit and tie – how to speak to other members of staff, how to dress, the importance of being punctual and so on.

Conversely, the Digital generations (with wealthier parents than we had) have spent their spare time doing more extra-curricular activities than you can shake a stick at, supported by conscientious parents. Those parents encouraged their children to take part in everything from Tae Kwon Do to learning the oboe. The intention was partly to make them more rounded individuals – and I'd say that has largely succeeded. It does mean that Digitals can lack work experience when they start their first post, though, so they are learning 'on the job' and developing their own sense of what work means.

If you're an Analogue manager and a fresh-faced graduate turns up for their first day without, in your eyes, a basic understanding of what is expected of them, recognise that they might just need a little more patience – and encourage your older staff members to deal with it patiently too.

Developing a management style for all generations

Each generation develops its own popular culture. Previously, when individuals have gone to work, they have had to leave that behind and conform to the traditional bureaucratic structure of organisations. In effect, that bureaucratic structure has become the default prevailing workplace culture. Today, the generational divide reflects the significant cultural and attitudinal differences between those who have grown up in a digital environment and those who have been exposed to rapid digital change later in life. This is complicated to manage.

These issues are different in every organisation and there is no single solution: managers need to acknowledge these intergenerational tensions when they happen, and deal with them. Don't allow conflict to fester, as it will affect the whole work environment and productivity.

As with all things, knowledge is power. So, let's revisit some of the key characteristics of each of these cohorts at work.

Baby Boomers

- Are more loyal to their employer and spend longer in a job

- Expect to be left to work independently without micromanagement

- Enjoy passing on their knowledge and experience

- Are used to working long hours and being at work on time – even when they are in poor health

- Expect recognition in the form of seniority and respect rather than praise

Generation X

- Are also quite happy to work independently and thrive on challenges

- Look to be given responsibilities

- Tend to challenge authority and the status quo more than Baby Boomers
- Expect to have a life outside of work
- Are keen on giving something back to their community

Millennials

- Want to achieve a better work/life balance than previous generations
- Expect plenty of feedback and encouragement
- Look for regular promotions
- Are content to find their own ways to do what they've been asked to do
- Are keener on social and corporate responsibilities than predecessor cohorts

Generation Y

- Are similar to Millennials but more extreme
- Alignment of social mission is important to them
- Need regular encouragement and feedback
- Require more guidance about expected workplace behaviour (including social media use while working)
- More integrated working and personal lives

Considering these (often quite conflicting) character-istics, it's easy to see why managing intergenerational teams can pose challenges. Most importantly, you need to discuss personal needs with each member of the team and manage them differently. In doing so, however, you also need to make sure you don't cre-ate schisms between members because they think one person (or group) is being favoured over another. When you take on a new employee, it's critical to talk to ask them the following questions:

- How much feedback do you want?

- How much of my time do you want or need?

- How do you want to communicate?

- How often do you want to communicate?

- How do you plan to keep me updated?

- What will kill your enthusiasm?

- What can I do to help you in your role?

These are especially relevant to the younger Digitals, who look for far more management input – but older workers may want your attention too!

'Six Tips for Motivating Millennials (BITC, 2019c) offers some excellent advice on strategies for keeping younger members of the team on board while reduc-ing potential intergenerational conflicts.

These include:

- **Make pay, benefits and promotions more transparent.** Research by Price Waterhouse Coopers (PwC) discovered that taking the mystery out of these decisions made employees more engaged and made it possible to fully acknowledge their contributions, both large and small (PwC, 2013).

- **Introduce group mentoring.** Satisfying Millennials' appetite for feedback can be time-consuming, but group mentoring encourages peer-to-peer support as a means of regular feedback. It also helps your business to develop a stronger sense of community and place more emphasis on teamwork, appreciation and support.

- **Invite Millennial employees to leadership meetings.** This allows them to shadow more experienced employees and see how decisions are made. This is especially helpful for employees who want to increase their skills while learning more about the business.

- **Allow Millennials to pitch personal projects that use their skills and knowledge.** This makes Millennials feel more engaged and in control of their careers, while boosting innovation in your business. It may also encourage older colleagues to get involved with these projects.

Management structure

We've already looked at the benefits of flatter structures in businesses. These allow you to hold on to talented older workers, who can work fewer days or move sideways, while enabling younger talent to shine through. But how can this work best in a multi-generational workplace? This example offers some possibilities:

CASE STUDY: OPPORTUNITIES FOR ALL

Soon after setting up Punter Southall Aspire, I recognised that some of the most talented younger leaders in our company were becoming frustrated. Having reached their late thirties and forties, they felt they had earned a seat at the top table. They were right – and they were ready for it. But there were just eight spots on our executive committee, most of which were occupied by equally talented and capable leaders who were a generation older than them.

To solve this problem, I disbanded the executive committee, replacing it with seven operational committees for different areas of the business. That way, we were able to quickly involve more people in our leadership structure while creating a more diverse, multi-generational team at the top.

As the UK workforce ages, you are likely to encounter this kind of dilemma more often. Your older employees may stay on board for longer, well past what was traditionally considered the 'retirement age' and into their seventies. Staff in that age group may have different skills, expectations and interests from those of Millennial workers, and even those who are in their forties. You need to find ways to help everyone work together in a productive way – and gain the full benefit of a multi-generational workforce.

Mentoring

How can you help your older workers pass on the knowledge and experience they have gained over decades to their younger colleagues, while encouraging younger colleagues to share their own unique knowledge with older employees?

Here's another example:

CASE STUDY: A CULTURE OF MENTORING

I worked with an older member of staff who had joined us after being made redundant with another firm. That company had been fairly 'old school' in their way of doing things, and the employee was used to having a secretary to handle all his appointments and room bookings. He found it hard to break that habit with us and instead use the software that everyone in the office was using. That was because he wasn't up to speed with technology.

Fortunately, someone (younger) spotted the problem and, discreetly, gave him a short coaching session to show how it was done. There was no fuss, and no embarrassment on his part that he had found it difficult to get to grips with a new way of doing things.

If you make it part of the culture in your business that people will recognise when someone is struggling to handle something new and step in to gently coach them, it will pay dividends. It operates both ways: younger workers can often spot that need and discreetly step in – equally, older workers will have experience of situations that younger members of team won't have dealt with. Not making anyone feel awkward about that is one of the big benefits of a multi-generational workforce.

KEY POINTS

1. Managers need to acknowledge intergenerational tensions when they happen and deal with them. Don't allow conflict to fester: it will affect the whole work environment and productivity.

2. Young people want evidence of purpose and social mission from their employer. They also see this as the way for a business to win and retain customers.

3. Digitals can lack work experience when they start their first post, because they tend not to have had many weekend or holiday jobs. They have to learn on the job and develop their own sense of what work means.

4. Invite Millennial employees to leadership meetings to shadow others and see how decisions are made. This is helpful for those who are looking to increase their skills while learning more about the business.

5. Make it part of your business culture for staff to recognise when someone of any age is struggling to handle something they haven't done before, and gently coach them through it.

SEVEN

Managing The Work-Life Balance

Why flexibility is here to stay

In March 2019, BNY Mellon told its 50,000 employees that they could no longer work from home (Hadfield, 2019). According to Chief Executive Charles Scharf, the bank believed that it would help collaboration to have more employees together in the same physical space.

The backlash from employees was fierce, with immediate threats of lawsuits. So was the reputational damage. MP Jo Swinson tweeted: 'I feel like sending a fax to BNY Mellon to tell them it's 2019… or maybe a carrier pigeon?' (Jo Swinson, 2019). Within forty-eight hours, Scharf had sent his staff an apologetic email telling them that he had 'listened and learned' to their concerns and would review the flexible working policy again.

Scharf had made one critical mistake, which every company – yours included – can learn from. Before I reveal that mistake, I should say that I fully understand CEOs and managers who want to curb flexible working. If you're from Generation X or older, the desire for flexible working can be mystifying. It just wasn't the done thing when we started our working lives.

In one of my first jobs, everyone had to be at their desks at 9am sharp – and all men had to have their ties on by 9.50am. Why? Because the boss turned up at 10am, and woe betide any staff member who wasn't present and looking the part. Many of my generation believe that you have to be sitting at your desk to be productive, and that you should come to the office dressed up rather than dressed down. We pat ourselves on the back for a job well done if we end the year without taking all our annual leave. Now that's dedication.

If I'm honest, I still enjoy this more formal way of working, as do many of our employees. But the younger generation see things differently. In one academic study, younger employees picked the top two factors that motivated them to stay in their jobs. Flexibility was the top choice, chosen by 59% (Smith & Galbraith, 2012). This was followed by proximity

(43%), enjoyable work (29%) and work environment (27%) (Smith & Galbraith, 2012). 'Work environment' includes not just where they work from – home, or perhaps a local cafe or library – but also the way they dress at work. They don't want to be forced into suits and ties.

Deloitte, in their 2017 Millennial Survey, found that in highly flexible working environments, only 38% of Millennial workers saw themselves leaving their job within two years and 31% expected to stay at least five years, a gap of 7% (Deloitte, 2017). In the least flexible organisations, the gap went up to 18%. The cohort that is following in their footsteps – Gen Z – is going to expect even greater levels of flexibility. In a survey powered by YouGov, one-third of 1,000 young people in the 17–23 age group said that a work-life balance was the most important factor after pay when choosing a job (CBI, 2018).

Digitals don't want to work a traditional nine to five. They want to make the most of their lives outside work, and if that means coming in late some mornings so they can spend the previous evenings enjoying themselves, that can matter more than a pay rise. They'll take all the leave available to them – and ask to buy more or request a sabbatical. It's easy to condemn the younger generation as slackers who aren't committed enough to their work. But that is not the case. They simply work differently.

Back to Charles Scharf: his mistake was to assume that he could change the people working for him so that they would look at work in the same way he did. But that train has long since left the station: that expectation of flexibility among employees is now ingrained. They have grown up with technology that allows them to work from anywhere, at any time. Digitals thrive on this technology – it's part of their DNA. If you are going to recruit and retain these younger workers, you need to work with this characteristic, not try to fight it.

Older workers love flexibility too

Managing a multi-generational workforce doesn't mean offering perks to one part of your team and not to the other. Fortunately, some benefits will please everyone.

In particular, that applies to flexibility. Mercer's 2017 Global Talents Survey showed that 51% of UK employees (across all age groups) wanted more fluid work options. Making that happen is critical if you want to harness the talents of a huge swathe of people who are leaving the workforce. One reason that people are leaving is caring responsibilities. Research by Carers UK (2019) showed that 2.6 million people have left their job to care for a loved one who is older, disabled or seriously ill, and nearly half a million (468,000) of those have left their job in the last two years. That's more than six hundred people a day, and it's a 12% increase since Carers UK and YouGov polled the public in 2013 (Carers UK, 2019). The findings also show that five million people are trying to juggle their job with caring – a huge leap from the 2011 figure of three million (Carers UK, 2019). The research, says Carers UK (2019, p5), 'emphasises the need for employers to support the rapidly increasing number of staff with caring responsibilities to stay in the workforce'.

Many of these staff are part of the 'sandwich generation' – people who are caring for parents and their children at the same time. Some even fall into what I've heard described as the 'club sandwich generation' – if you're in your fifties and sixties, there's a good chance that you've got grandchildren to worry about too. At a time when the social care system in this country is descending into crisis, children of ageing parents are anxious about leaving them to the tender mercies of an overstretched care worker for fifteen minutes a day. Unless you can build some flexibility into their working life, it could be that some of *your* older workers will join the six hundred a day who are quitting their jobs. And that's before we talk about older workers who have long-term health conditions or simply like the look of the work-life balance they see younger people striving for. In fact, research by BITC (2019a) has shown that nearly 40% of workers in the 55–59 age group want to reduce their working hours.

Whatever you do, once you have granted your personnel some degree of flexible working, it is not easy to reverse course. That means it's critical to get it right from the start. We'll look at this in the section on managing flexibility.

Your legal obligations

Even if you haven't written flexible working into your HR policies, all employees can actually ask for it as individuals. That right was established in 2014 under the Flexible Working Regulations. It includes asking for different hours, working from home and job-sharing.

The employee must have been working for the same employer for at least twenty-six weeks, they must make their request in writing, and they can only make a particular request once in a year. What's more, when they make their request, the employee has to set out what effect they think it would have on the business. It's not exactly a slam dunk.

Moreover, you are entitled to say no to the request. But you are legally obliged to deal with it 'in a reasonable manner'. This means considering the request carefully, meeting the employee to discuss it and offering them the chance to appeal if you turn their request down.

It's up to you to decide whether your business can cope with that person's request – and the others that may well follow. In particular, you need to consider whether you might lose the employee permanently by saying no, and if that's a risk worth taking. Or, you could take the opportunity to stand back, look at the bigger picture and develop a company-wide HR strategy around flexibility that lets everyone know where they stand. This can be the starting point for developing ways of working in your company that make the most of the benefits of agile working. We'll look at this more in the section on managing flexibility.

Types of flexible working

The main options to consider are as follows:

Flexitime: where employees fit their working hours around core office times. This is a good option if you want to avoid rush-hour commutes or give people the option to do the school run.

Annualised hours: working a set number of hours across the year that will meet your company's needs.

Restructured hours: compressing the working week so employees can, for example, do a four-day week without reducing the total number of hours they work.

Working reduced hours: for example, by working part time, job-sharing or working in term time. This can also include 'winding down' towards retirement by allowing employees to gradually cut down the number of hours they work.

Career breaks and sabbaticals: these allow people to take an extended holiday, do a qualification or pursue a personal ambition, such as writing a book or going on a pilgrimage. This option is becoming more popular.

Managing flexibility

Flexibility has been around a long time, especially in some service sectors, but UK office culture has taken a long time to catch up.

As someone in sales, I've always enjoyed a certain level of freedom because I've had clients to visit. When I had a young family and was living in Winchester, it always suited me to get up super early, get the early train to London and clock off at four. Instead of staring across a crowded commuter train at each end of the day, I could see my young children for bath time and story time. My manager was OK with that, because he could see that there was no negative impact on my performance. But I used to get a huge amount of flak from the rest of the office when I clocked off earlier than everybody else.

In London a certain amount of flexibility has always been expected because the public transport is unreliable. Not having to go through the rush-hour crush is also appealing, and the cost of commuting at peak hours is a consideration for some too. But it's understandable that, historically, companies haven't been that accommodating. It isn't that easy if you're trying to deal with customers who won't appreciate you being short-staffed at certain times of the day. You have to think about resources and who's going to fill the gaps that other people might leave. There's also a big issue of trust – and, in some cases, control.

When I've bought regional IFA businesses, which typically have a couple of dozen staff and one Baby Boomer owner, I've found that some have elected to 'control the business' by having everyone in the office five days a week, from 9am to 5pm, where they can see what they are doing. As we get more involved in running their company, and bring their business in line with the rest of our operation, sometimes it's not easy to persuade them to work differently.

'How do I know they're doing their job?' they demand.

'Well, why did you hire them if you don't feel you can trust them?' I retort.

Introducing flexible working

If you accept that your staff are routinely going to work from out of the office or outside office hours, give them the tools they need to do their job. Provide laptops, not desktops, store documents in the Cloud, and use Skype. If they are hotdesking, have software that allows people to book desks as well as offices in advance. One small caveat: while laptops may be the best option in most cases, that won't be so if they need to run demanding applications. Having PCs that staff can plug their devices into when they come into work might be part of the solution; so too is equipping staff with higher-spec equipment to work on when they're at home.

If that sounds expensive, remember that the cost of IT has dropped dramatically in recent years. It's also a relatively small overhead compared with those of hiring and keeping good personnel.

Flexibility can also extend to allowing people to work how they work best. If that means spending some time in a coffee shop with their headphones on rather than sitting at their desk, as long as they do the biz, why not? Ultimately, recognise that a better work-life balance is a good thing, which we can all benefit from. It should not be the preserve of younger workers only, and flexibility is a major step towards achieving that balance.

Think agile as well as flexible

So far, we've talked about the benefits of doing things differently from the perspective of employees. Now let's turn this on its head and look at how a more flexible workplace is the starting point for a more agile one – which can be hugely beneficial for employers.

Agile working practices are about using technology to create new ways of working. It takes flexible working to a new level by making it your preferred business model, with more people regularly working from home and virtual teams handling projects. In theory, as well as creating a happier (and more motivated) workforce, you can radically reduce the cost of your business space. If fewer people turn up on most days and hotdesking is the norm, you can trim the amount of space you rent and make your precious car-parking spaces go further. In some locations, these are sizeable business overheads. You can also serve your client base in ways that not only maintain your quality of service but also make it more responsive to their needs.

Many people are surprised that the service they're currently receiving from a provider doesn't come from a corporate office but is delivered via technology that spreads the load to where it can best be handled – whether that's satellite offices or even people working from home. That applies to everything from care workers and sales call handlers to global law firms whose clients are served twenty-four hours a day by a string of teams across the world.

Agile working has to be technology-led and, along with hotdesking and laptops, unified communications and collaboration platforms such as Slack or Skype for Business are essential. It's also important that employees can access files and data securely via the Cloud, rather than carrying about a laptop holding sensitive information. This technology means that providing seamless customer service by a highly agile team is now readily achievable.

Managing remote teams

Once you have more people working in teams remotely as well as (or instead of) in the office, you need to manage them so that you get the best out of them. Ultimately, this comes down to communications and trust – and establishing clear lines about what outcomes you expect from everyone in a team.

Not every manager is comfortable with this new way of working. It's not just about the sector you're in. My software manager, for example, prefers to have his team in one place where problems or queries can be shared and solved by bringing the chairs together. He argues that if you're in different locations it takes longer to set up shared screens – and you don't get the same conversations because you're not in the same room. I have had to encourage this manager to try a mixed working approach, so he can get to see the benefits without immediately giving up on his beliefs. That's from someone in technology. But, like countless other managers, he is having to come to terms with more virtual type teams, so you may have to spend more time coaching and supporting these managers as they change to the new way of working.

And how about the multi-generational aspect of all of this? Ironically, once Gen X and Boomers get past the novelty of working from home for some or all of their time, rather than religiously doing the daily commute, they are well equipped. After all, they are much more comfortable with working on their own, and they don't need regular reassurance that they're on track. It's the Millennials and Gen Zs who are keener on social interaction – they want to be part of a community – so they need more collaboration time than older workers. That means it's important to get the technology in place and achieve the right level of personal interaction.

My technology manager does have a point: screens and conference calls can only go so far. If you're going to foster the interchange of ideas, you have to create moments when you all come together – part-social, part-business – as an organised event. This helps people to develop trust and reach the point where they enjoy working with each other and understand each other.

Here are some ways to make remote teams more effective:

1. **Establish terms of reference for the team.** Goals, objectives and so on are even more important than usual, because extra time away from the office gives people time to forget.

2. **Hold regular face-to-face meetings with the whole team.** This will help them to collaborate and work together.

3. **Avoid misunderstandings.** Be more thorough with meeting notes and written communication so that there is less chance of misinterpretation.

4. **Provide quality time.** Encourage team members to spend time together in small groups or managing smaller projects. This encourages more sharing and collaboration in the team.

5. **Improve communication.** Use technology to encourage an ongoing dialogue that team members can dip in and out of.

6. **Hold events.** Have a bigger budget for team-building and social events to help replace the missing office environment.

KEY POINTS

1. More than six hundred people a day are leaving their jobs to care for a loved one, and five million employees are currently trying to juggle their job with caring.

2. If an employee asks to work flexibly, you are entitled to say no. But by law, you have to consider the request carefully, meet the employee to discuss it and offer them the chance to appeal against your decision.

3. Agile working practices use technology to create new ways of working. They make flexible working your preferred business model, with more people regularly working from home and virtual teams handling projects.

4. Gen X and Boomers are often comfortable working on their own from home – it's the Millennials and Gen Zs who are keener on social interaction, so they need more collaboration time.

5. To foster the interchange of ideas between remotely working teams, there have to be times when you all come together to develop trust and understanding.

EIGHT

Career Management

Different generations, different needs

To recruit and retain the most talented people, you need to ignore the date on their birth certificate. But if you are looking to assemble and keep a workforce that includes the best of all generations, you should recognise that not everyone is driven by the same things.

Traditionally, most people have gone to work firmly focused on generating 'financial assets'. When my generation entered work, we wanted security, good pay, a decent pension, and to become homeowners. Our ambition was to work our way up the ladder – and receive more financial assets. As such, Generation X and Baby Boomer managers naturally assume that younger cohorts want the same sort of things – to get paid enough to lead a decent life, accumulate wealth, support their families, buy a house, and eventually retire with enough to live in comfort and with dignity.

But survey after survey tells us that the Digital generation has its eyes set on a lot more than financial assets. They want a good work-life balance. That pushes financial assets down their list of priorities. They are also looking at a far different time horizon than that of the Analogue generations, who set their retirement alarm clocks for somewhere in their sixties. And they don't assume that they'll be with the same employer for long, or that they'll even be doing the same sort of job.

Today, workers need another type of asset – a class of asset which has nothing to do with money. And you, their employer, can provide it for them. I'm talking about what Gratton and Scott, authors of *The 100-Year Life* (2016), call 'intangible assets'. These are the skills and resources that will help people survive and thrive when they live longer than ever before – perhaps working into their seventies and even beyond. This could take them into a time when many of today's jobs will have been replaced by new ones, and when automation and artificial intelligence will have transformed the workplace.

Intangible assets

When people lived to sixty-five, seventy-five or eighty, their lifespan could be divided into three distinct phases – education, career and retirement. They spent most of the middle phase, which lasted for around forty years, in a small number of companies, getting successive promotions and earning a living. As longevity increases, that middle work phase might last for fifty or even sixty years. And people's careers are following a more circuitous path. Instead of working for three or four companies over a lifetime, they may work for seven, eight or even more.

They might switch between departments far more often. They may be part of a fluid workforce, which goes from contract to contract (gig to gig) with their role (and pay) going up and down accordingly. They might stop work for a while to take another degree in their forties or fifties, switch careers altogether, go on a sabbatical to refresh themselves, move into part-time work (and then back again) when they have children or elderly parents to support, start their own business – and, in some cases, never retire at all.

Navigating that complex career path takes more than money. Workers also need the following intangible assets (Gratton & Scott, 2016):

- **Productive assets.** The skills, knowledge, reputation and professional networks which an individual needs to find interesting work over several decades.

- **Vitality assets.** Mental and physical wellbeing, a good work-life balance, and supportive relationships that allow people approaching the traditional age of retirement to continue to work.

- **Transformational assets.** The self-knowledge and diverse networks that help your staff go through personal changes and transitions.

Here's an example:

CASE STUDY: INTANGIBLE ASSETS

Greg is forty-nine, and earns a good living as an IT technician. He has been in the workforce since his early twenties, and will likely work for another twenty-five or even thirty years.

The skills he learned when he graduated from university are a little rusty. He is scared that he is falling behind his younger colleagues, the digital natives. And sometimes, work has begun to feel stale and boring. He's been doing it for so long. IT was always his passion, but he needs a change of direction. He's just not sure what his professional options are.

Greg could really use help brushing up on his IT skills. This should probably be an ongoing programme of learning, because the knowledge he gains today will be out of date in a few years. He could also benefit from some variety in his job. His employer could give him new tasks, or help transfer his skills to other areas. And he would find the transition easier to figure out with a better professional network, which could give him new role models and help him recognise alternative options.

Cultivating lifelong learning, bringing variety to employment, and supporting individuals' capacity to transform – these are just some of the ways you can help your employees develop their intangible assets. You might also help them in their personal life by considering the needs of dual-income families. In today's stressful world, family and friendships are assets. You could give people the time and flexibility in their work schedule to build up those assets.

It's in your interests to do so, because you need your workforce to stay highly skilled, engaged, resilient and healthy if you want to stay competitive. In any case, before long, you will have no choice. Good candidates are likely to prioritise workplaces that can help them develop these skills and acquire these assets, because they will become every bit as vital as salary. The traditional career structure is evolving, and the workplace has no choice but to evolve with it.

How is your business going to help your workers develop more intangible assets? You need to think hard about this, and consider ways of developing a culture of lifelong learning, because you may need to shift talented people from one role in your company to another (that hasn't been invented yet). And when a highly promising person comes along for an interview, they'll be asking what you can do for them to progress their future and improve their life if they come and work for you – on top of paying them a decent salary.

Fluidity is the new norm

I've talked already about how many companies, including mine, are using a flatter structure. That, to me, has to be the way forward to accommodate a workforce that includes three or four generations. Many of those employees will be starting to plan beyond today's usual retirement age – taking breaks, acquiring new skills and refreshing their career along the way. A flatter structure is more fluid: it allows you to constantly reallocate staff to new teams as new projects come in the door, move them across departments to acquire new skills, or restructure as technology makes one set of jobs redundant and replaces them with another.

But with fluidity, there has also to be a conversation around salary. Companies can't always keep paying you more and more simply because of the years you've spent with them: you're only worth what you're worth. If you take a step sideways or even backwards, with it comes a drop in salary. That might sound harsh on the employee, but it's simply a step on from the project or fixed-term contract arrangements that many of us now work under. Moreover, this way of working does offer advantages for the individual: we're no longer looking at a steady climb in our careers, but a series of sprints and jogs. No matter what stage you are at in your life and career, you can elect to step back; and while that has obvious attractions for someone later in their career, it can also be helpful for a younger person who is seeking a better work-life balance.

Many larger enterprises already have this sort of structure built in, but smaller ones may not. It happened in my company because it grew so quickly: we've created job families, which individuals can hop between.

'Job hopping' is something the Digital generation is comfortable with. They're quite prepared to change companies when it suits them. If you have a fluid structure, you're allowing them to do that inside your operation, which helps you to retain the best people. However, these things don't happen by themselves: key to enabling this is to provide the training to reskill your people, and to put mentoring front and centre. This is yet another argument for creating a truly multi-generational workforce: the mentoring will work both up and down the age spectrum.

While many younger people may be happy with this fluidity, the more ambitious ones will absolutely want to know how their career is mapping out, and how many years it will take to get up the management ladder. That means you need to explain clearly what they need to do to progress: 'You want to reach this position – to do that you're going to need these skills, and to help you achieve that, I'm going to get you to do these tasks. And if you're successful, I will recommend that you will be promoted.' You also need to have regular conversations with them to track their progress, so there's no doubt in that person's mind about what to expect.

Gen X and Boomers haven't been managed in that way in the past, so it's far more of a surprise for them. Again, that means you need to explain your approach carefully and manage expectations.

Retention strategies need to change

CASE STUDY: JAMES

You hired James right out of university. He's the best and brightest of his peers. He worked hard, was promoted quickly, and out-performed nearly all of his colleagues.

But when he hit his late forties, after working non-stop for twenty-five years, he began itching for something new. He wanted to travel, expand his horizons, maybe start up a new business and spend more time with his family.

You begged him not to leave, but he resigned, with no other work lined up.

Every company has cases like this: of star employees whom you cultivate, nurture and rely on – and then suddenly they leave to do something radically different, or just take time out. There is a crucial lesson for your business: ensuring your recruitment process does not overlook well-qualified but older candidates is not enough if you can't *keep* the best talent. And as we live for longer – and work for longer – that becomes increasingly challenging.

The traditional career structure is changing. The stability of full-time work, with high salaries and regular promotions, followed by retirement at age sixty-five, simply isn't as attractive as it once was. Instead, workers like James, in the middle of their careers, want to try out different career paths, take on new challenges, take time out and then return to the workforce renewed and refreshed, and to find a good work-life balance. When they do reach the traditional retirement age, they are often keen to continue working – whether in their existing position, shifting to part time, or taking on a new role altogether.

This cohort still has decades of experience and wisdom to offer – if only they still feel supported and welcome. To keep our best employees, we have to adjust to these new realities. We must think harder about how to support employees of every age, as their work patterns and needs change. We need to consider how to create workplaces which are age-diverse, and where the company can gain all the benefits of having a more flexible, older workforce.

Here are some starting points:

- **Introduce a mid-career review for staff in their forties.** This will help them to analyse where they would like their career to go and make plans accordingly.

- **Broaden your range of career trajectories.** Introduce more options for flexible, part-time and remote work.

- **Train your managers.** Be proactive about training managers to support workers of all ages and skill levels, initiating additional management training as needed.

- **Be transparent.** Be open about the age demographics in your company, so that any potential biases or age-related issues can come to light. Ideally the age demographic of your business should match your client base.

- **Introduce mentoring.** Match younger and older workers so they can mentor each other, sharing their knowledge and skills.

Lifelong learning and the seven ages of work

In the truly multi-generational workplace, one where each person might perform multiple roles over a period, what differences will there need to be in their career development?

Let's start with what we know – or rather, how we've been taught – because that does shape the way we approach work.

The Digital generation has been hot-housed in their education – constantly set milestones, their child-hoods punctuated with testing and rewards. They have an expectation that when they come to work this will continue: mapped out in front of them will be a series of tasks, steps and rewards. The rewards can be a public 'well done', a bonus, a pay rise or a change in job title. But it's important to map out the path to achieving them and to follow this through with regular career meetings. In these, you can discuss their progress: are they doing the right things, achieving their objectives, on target for being CEO in twenty years?

Contrast this with when I started work: we had an annual appraisal, which occasionally led to a pay rise and (even less occasionally) a promotion. And that was it – unless you didn't do something well, when you were taken to task.

To manage the expectations of the Millennials in my business, I hold monthly one-to-ones. In these, we discuss what's gone well and what hasn't in the last four weeks, and set out my expectations and theirs for the coming month. Importantly, this provides the opportunity to flag up the need for extra training or coaching that will help them achieve their objectives – and yours.

As a Gen X, I'd find it exasperating to be micro-managed in that way. And it's not the way I do it with John, my Boomer-generation head of marketing. We still have a monthly one-to-one, but the content is not the same – it's far more task-driven. Digitals need more handholding, and Analogues want more of a collaborative conversation. But it's important to hold monthly meetings with everyone in your team: these one-to-ones are at the core of how you manage your intergenerational workforce, and you can flex the content to meet the needs of the individual.

Mid-life career reviews

If retaining the talents and experience of older people in the workforce is important for the economy, for companies and for the individuals themselves, how we can we make sure that they take the right course to meet their needs and aspirations?

In 2006, careers professionals and labour market researchers suggested that it would be advantageous for workers to step back when they turn fifty or so and review their options – primarily in the workplace, but also considering other aspects of their life (NIACE, 2015). The idea was that it would help individuals to understand their rights, the opportunities for staying in work and the financial risks of retiring early. The idea was developed by the National Institute of Continuing Adult Education, with others. In 2013, pilot services were tested with about three thousand people. That was the beginning of an initiative which, if undertaken properly, could change the landscape for the workplace. It has become known as the mid-career review, although it's sometimes referred to as a mid-life MOT.

The concept gained support in 2017 when John Cridland set out his independent review of the State Pension age (Cridland, 2017), much of which was based on the premise that we need to keep people economically active for longer. This review recommended that mid-career reviews should be a standard part of the HR landscape. The next stage was to run some pilots. Each pilot was run slightly differently by different companies, which included L&G and Aviva. They were then reviewed by the Centre for Ageing Better (2018), the Lottery-funded charity set up to improve older people's lives by establishing 'what works'.

The review of the pilots demonstrated that there is a real appetite among people approaching the later years of their working life to have a frank, in-depth discussion about the interlinking aspects of their future: their wellbeing, their finances and their work options. The concept works for businesses too: the companies I have discussed it with all think it is an excellent concept, though all of them already hold regular career reviews with all their staff.

Where the mid-career review adds more value than a career review is that it really goes into depth. It starts with a person's finances: calculating when they can afford to retire or reduce their working hours, and how much more they need to save. It also gives them a health check as part of the Mid-Life MOT to put their work-life balance into perspective. Then it dissects what they need to do, and what they could do, to get the most out of the rest of their working life.

There's an argument that discussions around work should be held with an outsider. Just how frank will a person be with their line manager if they suspect the manager wants to make them redundant? A solution might be to use a consultant or the government-funded careers service and money advice service. Nevertheless, I expect the mid-career review to become a standard tool in the HR toolbox over the coming years, driven by forward-looking businesses like L&G and Aviva rather than relying on government support.

Winding down

CASE STUDY: MARK

Mark is fifty-five and came to my company after an acquisition. He'd been working in a senior role – with all that entailed in hours and pressure. When his company made the move to us, this opened up an opportunity for Mark to have a conversation about the future.

He's subsequently stepped down a couple of rungs, does a four-day week, and leaves at 5pm. That suits him now... but it certainly wouldn't have suited him ten years ago when he was still looking up the ladder.

Me? I'm delighted. He's still in the business – with all the experience and knowledge he has acquired. Everything that's happened in this sector in the last twenty years is in his head.

Without a conversation like that, there's a danger that someone like Mark will either leave the business voluntarily or get pushed aside because they're seen as an obstacle to the thrusting young executives coming up behind them. This is just one example of winding down – something that's become more popular but is still not as ubiquitous as it should be. And one size of winding down doesn't fit all.

A few years ago, another senior colleague, Alan came to me. He was approaching sixty and had been reflecting on the fact that he had been working for over forty years. In that time, he had been fortunate to have never been out of work and even more fortunate to (so far) have had virtually no time off due to illness. Although he had had a full working life, he wasn't yet ready to stop work because he was in an exciting company with some great plans for the future, which he wanted to see come to fruition. That said, the pace was relentless at times, and occasionally he found it hard to think straight.

Concerned that he may have to come off the pace at some point in the future, he was considering whether a four-day week would be the right thing. He couldn't explain how he'd fit his job into a four-day week though, which would be one of the requirements for anyone asking for flexible working. We discussed giving him more holidays, but that still posed problems.

What we came up with was a two-month sabbatical. This would give him the time to achieve some of the long list of life targets that were stacking up, with every year that passed making the physically demanding ones more remote. He went away, ticked off some boxes and came back feeling fired up and refreshed. He told me afterwards that towards the end of the two months, he was feeling completely reinvigorated and ready to return to work.

One common symptom of ageing is an increasing sense of your own mortality. If you're going to be working until you're seventy or older, why not take time out to cycle round Italy, stay on a kibbutz or drive the Pacific Highway? A sabbatical gives you the freedom to get that out of your system and achieve your dream while you physically can. From the employer's perspective, it reduces the chance of someone leaving, burning out after a few more years, or getting ill.

It's really important to have regular conversations to cover this sort of ground. As far as is realistic, you need to be flexible enough to accommodate the person's needs. Equally, you need to have a company culture which acknowledges that to wind down, your senior people – who were brought up in a hierarchical system – can move across, sideways or even downwards without losing status in the business, even if that means changing job titles so that employees can maintain the prestige of a certain role. The flipside is that there has to be a discussion about money. This is where many companies' HR polices have not yet caught up. I have found the only solution is an informal, open and honest conversation about the individual's future ambitions, which includes the financial consequences of any changes. You need to give your HR policies softer edges, without exposing yourself to people who would take advantage of you.

KEY POINTS

1. The Digital generation wants a good work-life balance. That pushes financial rewards down their list of priorities.

2. They are looking to develop skills that will help them thrive when they get older – perhaps working beyond their seventies in a time when many of today's jobs won't exist.

3. Instead of working for two or three companies in a lifetime, people may work for seven, eight or even more, with breaks and career changes in between.

4. Cultivating lifelong learning, bringing variety to employment and supporting individuals' capacity to transform are just some of the ways you can help your employees develop their intangible assets.

5. It's in your interests to be more flexible, because you need your workforce to stay highly skilled, engaged, resilient and healthy if you want to stay competitive.

NINE

Coaching And Mentoring

The building blocks of intergenerational teamworking

A London-based organisation called The Age of No Retirement (TANR), working with some of the biggest UK businesses, has developed a compelling narrative for breaking down the long-established habit of stereotyping people at work because of their age. Age, they maintain, does not define us.

In their words: 'The future is people-centric and post demographic; in other words, age-neutral and intergenerational' (TANR, 2019). Of course, there are nuances here to be teased out. Our age is one of the things that inevitably does shape our thinking and approach to life. We are, at least in part, moulded by the world we grew up in, and by the physical and mental changes that come with growing older. But other factors can be just as meaningful: our education, parents, political views and religious beliefs.

How does this play out in the workplace? What is the best way to harness the talents of people of all ages?

According to research carried out by TANR (Hall & Williams, 2019), 83% of people want to mix with those of different ages. And according to Randstad (2019), 86% of employees believe that working in an intergenerational team can help promote innovation, which I see as a real plus point if we are seeking to create a truly intergenerational workforce. Indeed, according to TANR (2019), 'Wisdom and experience combined with the innovation and dynamism of youth make for powerful team performance.' They advocate for 'diverse, blended, intergenerational teams to become the norm, not the exception'. These teams should 'be built in accordance with skills and capabilities, not hampered by stereotypes and misperceptions'.

Intergenerational working is nothing new, but it usually happens in a hierarchical way – with the owner, managing director or finance director at the top (often in their fifties or sixties), the senior executives one level down (in their forties or fifties), followed by middle managers (in their thirties and forties), and junior personnel (in their twenties). There might also be some lower ranked older people performing less demanding roles. I am talking about something different: consciously building a team of (possibly widely) different ages to work together in complementary roles. This could be on a project or location basis, or it could be company-wide.

The word 'team' here is the key. In an intergenerational team, the team members are not artificially defined or divided by age; it is their talent that is important. The employer recognises that each member can bring something unique to a team and then nurtures that talent. In doing so, the employer makes sure that the experience and life skills of older people aren't lost, and that the energy, enthusiasm and creativity of young people is allowed to blossom.

There shouldn't be any resistance to making that happen in your workplace, as long as you consider the following key components:

- **Create a nurturing environment.** In that environment, people can learn from each other, respect each other's differences, find common ground and appreciate what they each bring to the party.

- **Support individual members.** Make sure managers understand the life situation and motivations of each individual in that team and can provide the support they need to achieve what *they* want in their career.

- **Create workplaces where people of all ages feel happy to work.** Consider adjusting the physical environment and allowing people to work away from the office.

- **Break down barriers.** Aim for people to understand each other, feel free to share their ideas and thoughts, and reach out for help when they need it.

- **Set team goals and roles.** Recognise the assets that each member brings, and involve them in selecting new members as the team grows or someone leaves.

- **Cement the concept of mentoring.** Encourage employees in different generations to share their skills and knowledge.

- **Support individuals.** Build continuous development and lifetime learning into every aspect of the company's business.

Preserving and transferring experience

Every morning, Christine Lucas wakes up with no memory of the day before. No matter what she did, who she spoke to, what she watched or what she read, she has no memory of it. Every time she wakes up, it's a blank slate. She realises that she needs to find alternative ways to remember things. She starts recording a daily video and writing a diary, so she can retain her knowledge from one day to the next.

That's the basic premise of SJ Watson's book *Before I Go To Sleep*, a psychological thriller that was made into a movie starring Nicole Kidman. This fiction is reminiscent of the modern workplace, because businesses also have a problem with retaining knowledge. People change jobs more frequently than they used to, taking with them all the knowledge they have gained about how to do their job, the company and its client history. That can be a big loss to any organisation, especially when staff turnover is high. For those companies, constant reinvention is critical – just as it was for Christine Lucas.

Once upon a time, the knowledge and skills you gained in university stayed relevant for decades. Nowadays, given the speed of technological and societal change, the skills required to do a job are constantly evolving… and the way things were done just a few years ago are easily forgotten. According to the 2018 *LinkedIn Workplace Learning Report* (Lefkowitz et al., 2018), the average lifespan of a skill is now less than five years.

There are no longer jobs for life, so the best skills to have in your company may not be highly specific or specialist at all. Instead, they may be softer, transferable skills such as teamwork, communications, flexibility, calmness under pressure, customer handling, problem-solving and leadership. And because the knowledge required to do a job changes so frequently, it no longer always makes sense to promote those who have the most experience – at least not in a specialism. Increasingly, teams are headed by people with the best managerial skills, sometimes even professional managers. Team members, therefore, can no longer assume that their boss can teach them the skills they need to do their job.

With that in mind, we need to find new ways to pass on knowledge so we can learn new skills quickly and retain memories that are otherwise in danger of being forgotten. That is why, as our workforce ages, transferring knowledge from one generation to the next will become a key activity. Younger workers will look to older workers for their organisational memory. Having people around with longstanding client relationships, who can remember best practices developed over years and who can provide some continuity with the past, will help businesses function smoothly at a time of rapid change.

Older workers may look to younger workers to help them keep up to date with modern skills and technical knowledge. Realistically, though, continuing education will be a priority for everyone, regardless of their age. According to the Association for Talent Development, the US equivalent to the CIPD (Manorek, 2019):

To stay competitive, organizations must have a plan for both upskilling and reskilling their employees and have an established and supported learning culture to keep teams engaged in ongoing employee development.

Enhancing the learning cycle

According to HR guru Josh Bersin (2018), 'The single biggest driver of business impact is the strength of an organization's learning culture.' A learning culture doesn't mean sending staff on the odd training day, as useful as that can be. It's something that has to be woven into the warp and weft of everything we do.

In my business, every month, each team holds a session where everything – and anything – can be discussed. These are seen as an important part of the month: our younger employees crave them, while older staff see them as helpful practical sessions. I certainly find some big cultural differences between what people are prepared to talk about: the younger generation, versed in sharing their lives on social media, are much more open about what they will discuss. Analogues like me tend not to share private stuff at work unless it's with a friend, but Digitals don't seem to have that filter.

It dawned on me a couple of years ago that if we were to become tighter as a team, we needed to understand each other – and that was one of the things I learned from Millennials. To help with this, I introduced the 'sign in' at the beginning of the monthly meeting, which I mentioned in Chapter 5. Each person gives their personal life, professional life and wellbeing a score out of ten. It's an opportunity for them to explain what's gone well and what problems they've had. It's not compulsory to go into detail, but as time has gone on, everyone has entered into the spirit of it.

Starting the meeting with a personal reflection breaks down reserve and sets the tone for the meeting; then, when you reach the business section, people are much more transparent and responsive, and the meeting is far more productive. It also creates better understanding of what other pressures people in the team are dealing with in their lives. This can reduce disagreements and tensions, heading potential rifts off at the pass. Knowing what issues they are facing also gives you insights into how to manage individuals in that team.

Because it forces reflection, it can often lead to changes in business strategies. It flushes out task-related problems and drives collaborations and teamwork: as soon as someone flags up that they are finding part of a task beyond them, others step up and offer to help. It is also a powerful reminder that every business has to incorporate continuous development and lifelong learning. That eye-opening experience led directly to another component being added to each meeting:

we now take it in turns to select a TED talk to watch together, and then discuss what we've learned from it and whether we could apply anything in the business.

Watching a TED talk is learning, but it's not going off and doing a training course. It happens regularly enough to deal with problems that are just starting to bubble, or the team have not even considered facilitating time to discuss, and allowing you to come collectively to a view on something. Interestingly, it also highlights generational differences – one person's 'greenwashing' can be really important to someone else. Most importantly, though, it's an opportunity to have a frank dialogue about a topic without it feeling contrived: it's a third party giving their views and individuals providing their take on them. It's also revealing to see what TED talks each person selects: rather like the records they'd take with them to a mythical desert island, it says something about them.

When I started work, we had monthly sales meetings, but they were one-way bureaucratic blasts from the top: these are the numbers, this is how you're going to achieve them. Now, we've got project groups, a manager thinking about generational conflicts, personal concerns being raised, collective learning, a collaborative approach. It's light years from the way things used to be done... thank goodness.

These meetings really are super-productive, with everyone providing, and being open to, new ideas.

In addition, by sharing failures or problems, and collectively looking for solutions, each person learns from others without points being scored.

That's why the age diversity of your team is massively important: if it was just Baby Boomers or Millennials in the room, it would be a vastly different experience.

Mentoring works for every generation

I come from a sales background, and there is a long tradition in this discipline of the best salesperson being promoted to sales manager. That can often work well – but not always.

Many great salespeople are so good because if you put them in front of a customer, they know how to engage with them and close the sale. That's a fantastic skill, but it has nothing to do with managing people. Promote them and they can struggle with the people-management skills you need to coax the best out of a team. Back to football: the most skilful player doesn't necessarily make the best captain.

Speak to people from other disciplines and they will tell you the same: someone being the best at their job doesn't guarantee that they will make the grade if they're promoted, say from a journalist to an editor, or from a teacher to a head teacher. However, they might make that leap successfully if they are mentored in the role by someone with the life skills and experience to fill the gaps in their armour.

Older workers, no matter how up to date their technical skills are, will have tacit knowledge built up over decades. This can benefit their younger colleagues. Organisations that have preferred older workers to retire early should carefully consider whether they really want to give up so much human capital. Wouldn't it be better instead to create mentoring programmes, where mature staff can work side by side with younger employees and share their insights?

Mentoring does not necessarily have to be about direction; it can be about cooperation, and it can be fostered informally through social networks. You could consider moving mature workers to other areas of the organisation that could benefit from their expertise and knowledge. You might decide to create forums and platforms at work where knowledge can be exchanged and flourish. It is paradoxical, but the faster our knowledge evolves, the more important it becomes to learn from people who have 'been around the block'. This mentoring is just one of the many benefits of a genuinely age-diverse workforce.

For the older employee, that means being in an invigorating environment where they can learn things from younger members of the team and get a buzz from passing their experience on – being a mentor and a capacity-builder. For the younger employee, they are part of a nurturing environment where they can learn life skills and interpersonal skills from more experienced people. They can gradually move into new roles as older employees wind down, rather than finding themselves promoted beyond their capabilities.

Being good at your job doesn't mean that you're going to be a great manager. But you might just get there with mentoring to help you.

KEY POINTS

1. According to Randstad (2019), 86% of employees believe that working in an intergenerational team can promote innovation.
2. The average lifespan of a skill is now less than five years.
3. Increasingly, teams are headed by people with the best managerial skills. Sometimes they are even professional managers.
4. As our workforce ages, transferring knowledge from one generation to another will become a key activity. In turn, older workers may look to younger workers to help them keep up to date with new skills and technical knowledge.
5. To help businesses function smoothly in a time of rapid change, it's important to have people around who have longstanding client relationships, who can remember best practices developed over years and who can provide some continuity with the past.

TEN

Benefit And Reward Structures

How to attract and reward employees

As an employer who is looking to attract and retain a talented workforce – one that enjoys coming to work and is operating to maximum effectiveness – there's plenty you can do beyond paying a decent salary.

Ask yourself the following questions:

- What do I want my future workplace demographic to look like?

- How do I build a rewards and benefits package that will work for them… and for me?

For a start, it's important to understand your employees' needs and priorities when it comes to their

169

finances, wellbeing and life. You then need to help your staff achieve them, if it's in your power to do so. That's why it's so important to understand how intergenerational differences will affect those needs and priorities.

Let's start with money. And, for instance, let's consider Tom:

CASE STUDY: TOM

Ever since auto-enrolment, Tom has been putting money into his pension every month. It's still not at a level that everyone would like to see (15%), but it is going up. He also has a savings account, which he tops up whenever he has some spare cash. He's planning to use the money to buy a new kitchen.

Unfortunately, Tom doesn't put money in his savings account every month. That's because he likes spending on 'nice to haves' – after all, what would life be like without the occasional luxury or reward for a hard month's work? He worries that his spending occasionally gets out of control, which is why he hasn't yet been able to buy that new kitchen.

Can you guess how old Tom is likely to be?

My company recently surveyed 2,000 UK employees about their approach to money and savings (Nelson, 2018). Although there were many more similarities than differences across the age groups, those who were younger than forty-five and those who were older than forty-five sometimes displayed very distinctive attitudes. Understanding these subtleties can be important if you want to encourage your staff to take control of their financial futures.

So, how old is Tom? Of course, there are 'Toms' in every age bracket. However, our research showed that his financial behaviour was more typical of people under the age of forty-five: younger respondents to our survey were typically less 'financially disciplined' (as an old-fashioned bank manager might have expressed it, back in the days when you could actually speak to one). Even though they were more likely to have credit card debt or a loan other than their mortgage (59% versus 42%), respondents who were younger than forty-five were less likely to prioritise paying off that debt (49% versus 59%) (Nelson, 2018).

They were also more likely to spend money on buying new things (50% versus 40%) and more likely to spend on 'nice to haves' (42% versus 23%) (Nelson, 2018). Why? The most common answer among respondents younger than forty-five was 'to improve my life' (29%). Those who were older than forty-five were more likely to spend on luxuries when they wanted to do something nice for someone else (30%). Perhaps as a result, younger people were more likely to admit buying more than they could afford (54% versus 30%)

and to feel like their spending was out of control (16% versus 9%) (Nelson, 2018).

When it came to savings, younger people in our survey were actually more likely to put money into a workplace pension (71.6% versus 65.4%). Presumably, this is because they were automatically enrolled, or because older people were more likely to have a workplace pension from a previous job (51.5% versus 46.4%). And – going against conventional wisdom – both groups put aside money for other purposes at remarkably similar rates: 52% of older people saved regularly, compared with 53% of younger people (Nelson, 2018).

But there were differences across the age range in why – and how – they saved. Younger people were more likely to save for a specific objective, such as a house or holiday (23% versus 19%). They were less concerned with long-term security (31% versus 36%). They also preferred to save in bigger lumps (43% versus 31%), rather than making steady savings payments – perhaps because they are saving when the money is available, rather than on a consistent basis (Nelson, 2018).

What are the implications of this research for your company? Firstly, it supports common knowledge that if you want to encourage your employees to save more for their pension, you have to communicate with the younger ones differently from the older ones. We'll look at this in more detail in Chapter 11. But this survey shows that you need to make some other changes too. If your retirement is four or five decades away, you will have different financial priorities from someone whose retirement is a mere ten or fifteen years away. The younger people we spoke to are not against saving – most of them try their best to put money away. But they are more likely to save for short- or medium-term needs, as and when they have the money to do so. With that in mind, instead of pushing your younger employees to save more for their pension, you could offer them a blended savings solution.

For example, you could put your younger staff members' auto-enrolment contributions directly into a pension, but allow them to put the rest of their contribution (and yours) into an ISA, which they can use to save up for shorter-term goals. Someone like Tom would probably love to have you contribute towards his home improvements. Because he is less interested in or able to make steady payments into his savings account, an ISA that he can contribute to easily on an ad-hoc basis would probably suit him, too.

This money will probably never be put towards Tom's retirement, but it will get him into the habit of saving and help to ensure that he makes the most of his future, wherever that takes him.

Let's talk benefits

That's just one way in which you can make your employees happier. But there's so much more to think about nowadays.

As an Analogue, I started work in an era when you sought out employers who could offer you job security, the chance of promotion after four or five years, a company pension and (above all, for me) a company car – not forgetting a decent salary with annual increments. Today's new job hunters will not be expecting to stay in their job for more than a year or two, so job security isn't really an issue: if the company closes or makes redundancies, they're confident they can find work elsewhere. Promotion? If they don't get one within twelve or even as few as six months, they'll be looking elsewhere. Company pension? As they probably won't be staying that long, it's not an issue: they'll be signed up to auto-enrolment, which will move with them anyway. Company car? No one has one of those any more, except perhaps the top brass. Anyway, their city centre apartment doesn't have a parking space and the roads are congested, so they rely on public transport.

One thing that hasn't changed is that today's fresh-faced employee still wants a decent salary. But just as important to them will be the other benefits available, including:

- Travel insurance

- A discount card

- Critical illness and life insurance

- Gym membership

- The option to buy more holidays

- Generous maternity / paternity leave

- Flexible start and finish times

- The option to work from home one or two days a
  week

Other 'nice to haves' include telephone or online access to a GP or health adviser, free financial and debt advice, or a credit-builder card.

If the person you're interviewing happens to be in their forties, fifties, sixties or beyond, they'll be hoping for rather different benefits, such as:

- Private medical insurance

- A dental plan

- The chance to taper their retirement

They'll certainly be concerned about pension arrangements, because they'll want to build up enough contributions before they retire.

In my company, we spend our time advising employers about which benefits today's workers want, and what savings options and advice they're looking for. It's a vastly changed landscape from even a few years ago. But if you want to recruit and retain an intergenerational workforce, you really do need to understand what presses different people's buttons.

If you get this right, apart from recruiting and retaining the best people, you'll have a workforce that's giving its best. An analysis (Edmans, 2012) of the previous twenty-eight years of stock market data found that businesses with high levels of employee satisfaction outperform their peers by 2.3% to 3.8% a year (89% to 184%, cumulatively) in long-run stock returns. Of course, other factors influence employee satisfaction too – not least, a company's mission and values, which matter so much to younger employees. Grouped together, though, the benefits and rewards structure you offer will have a lot more weight.

The challenge of pensions

Many managers find it difficult to encourage some employees to take their pension pots seriously. There's still an assumption that a few hundred thousand pounds is a lot of money. But if you assume that you can only safely take 4% of that a year, £250,000 yields just £10,000 a year on top of a State Pension of just over £8,500. When you're worrying about other aspects of your finances and retirement seems a long way off, it might not be at the top of your mind.

Yet everywhere you look in the financial press, there are dire warnings that today's workforce is not saving enough for a comfortable retirement. For once, the press have got it about right: the decline of DB schemes means that the golden age of company pensions will soon be gone. Instead, defined contribution (DC) schemes are on the increase – mainly because of the introduction of auto-enrolment. While contribution levels started modestly enough, they are now rising to a slightly more sensible level at around 8% – although anyone in the pensions sector will tell you that a total contribution of 15% is closer to the ideal.

A lot of flexibility is built into auto-enrolment, mainly to accommodate the number of times people will move jobs in a lifetime of work. Most schemes allow you to transfer your pension pot to another pension scheme, which could be a new employer's workplace pension scheme, a personal pension scheme, a SIPP (self-invested personal pension) or a SHP (stakeholder pension scheme).

Employees have the option to increase their contributions beyond the minimum, and employers have the option to match that. If you match their contributions, that's a big incentive for someone who is keen to build their pot, regardless of their age. Those who are closer to retirement are far more likely to be enthusiastic about that option, though: younger staff will be more focused on clearing their debts or saving for a deposit on a house. There's another distinguishing factor, too: the Digital generation is much more aligned to values and missions. This is increasing demand for environmental, social and governance (ESG) funds. Their thinking is: 'If I'm going to save several hundred thousand pounds in my lifetime, I want it to make a difference.'

Increasingly, I'm providing advice that will help my clients' employees (of all ages) to enjoy the flexibility that's important in their life, but still have a decent pension pot at the end of their career. Having non-pension savings as well as pension savings gives employees that flexibility – for sabbaticals, for time off, to train for second career and so on. The ultimate tax benefit of your pension fund is that it is exempt from inheritance tax. By the time you die, you want to have exhausted all your other savings and just be left with your pension. Having other savings to fall back on rather than dipping into your pension pot helps you keep it intact. With that in mind, offering financial advice to employees as part of a mid-career review should be part of the employee benefits package because it can inform the rest of their working careers. Ideally, you would offer regular reviews rather than a one-off, as people's lives change. Seeing an IFA when you're at the point of retiring is a bit late in the day… especially if you've already taken money out of your pension pot.

Other benefits – and how different generations value them

Earlier in this chapter I listed some of the benefits that companies can offer to attract and reward employees. Bigger companies have been providing these for some time, but they are now starting to become standard for many SMEs. These benefits cost employers very little, but if you source them correctly they can deliver a lot of bang for your buck. It's important to know which benefits will appeal to whom, allowing you to tailor your packages to employees of different ages.

Private medical insurance. This has long been a staple benefit. If employees can receive treatment when it suits them, that helps employers as well as the employee. At a time when NHS waiting lists are lengthening, older employees really do appreciate private medical insurance to deal with long-term or serious medical issues, especially if they can add their partner to the package. The attraction for younger employees, who are generally more passionate about the NHS, is that it can provide speedy access to medical experts for sports injuries or just peace of mind about potential cancer issues.

Death in service benefit. Some companies still offer this. The payout is usually between two and four times the employee's annual salary. This too has considerable 'Analogue appeal'. Perhaps not surprisingly, the

179

younger generations don't see as much value in this benefit, as they tend to enjoy better health.

Insurance. Life insurance, and critical illness cover in particular, are big pluses for younger cohorts. They can use it as cover when they take out a mortgage, and they are becoming more aware of the cancer risks for younger people. Although older workers may not need life insurance, if it is required it is a cheaper route to cover without medical underwriting.

Cash plans. Plans that are linked to wellbeing are highly attractive to employees of all ages, and you can tailor them to the employee. Younger members of staff may appreciate a gym membership or access to sports injury therapists, while all employees may welcome free eye and allergy tests, a dental plan or access to a chiropractor.

Voluntary benefits. These provide discounts on food at restaurants and takeaways. They suit younger generation employees, not least because they are so easy to use through smartphone apps. They can cost you from as little as £50 a year.

Employee assistance programmes. These give employees telephone or Facetime access to advice about health – especially mental health. They are popular with employees in the younger generation, who are more comfortable with talking about their problems on the phone.

Buying holidays. During interviews with Millennial and Generation X candidates, a standard question these days is: 'Can I buy extra holidays?' Although that's not something an older candidate would automatically ask, they will still find it an attractive part of your HR policy if they are thinking of winding down or they know that care responsibilities are heading their way.

Give as you earn schemes. In these schemes, regular contributions are taken from the employee's salary and paid to a charity of their choice. These schemes are more attractive to the younger generation, who have societal values and whose work and personal life is more integrated. It also reduces their tax liability.

Debt advice and help. In the UK, 8.3 million people are unable to pay their debts or household bills (NAO, 2018). Some of them may be working for you, and suffering from the stress that debt brings. Often, they are people in their forties and fifties, sometimes in well-paid jobs, struggling to keep afloat after the mortgage, children's tuition fees and (quite possibly) maintenance payments go out the door.

Suppliers (for example, Neyber) can help them – and ultimately you – by providing money-management tools and payroll-deducted loans. This is a far better solution than high-interest loans or credit cards: it rebuilds their credit rating and gets them to the point where they can start saving for a pension. Again, this benefit costs you little but can make a big difference to the lives of your staff.

Flexibility. I've already explained why flexibility matters to all employees these days – albeit for different reasons. Because it's so important to all of them, flexibility has to be a big part of any company's benefits and rewards package – whether that's variable start and finish times, time off to provide care or retrain, or a sabbatical.

Your staff and potential recruits will need to know that – as an employer – you will be sympathetic to their requests. However, HR departments are traditionally averse to writing this into policies, because they fear that new employees will take advantage of them. If that's the case with your HR department, a good workaround is to state that you will fulfil everything expected of you under employment law and that you will treat every request sympathetically – but at the manager's discretion.

If you don't have any of these policies in place, how will a prospective employee know you will be open to considering their request – even if it's just the starting point for a discussion?

KEY POINTS

1. Businesses with high levels of employee satisfaction outperform their peers by 2.3% to 3.8% per year (89% to 184% cumulative) in long-run stock returns (Edmans, 2012).

2. For younger employees, just as important as a decent salary are benefits that can improve their work-life balance and help them save money – among others, a discount card, critical illness and life insurance, gym membership, or the option to buy holidays.

3. Other 'nice to haves' are telephone or online access to a GP and health adviser, free financial and debt advice, or a credit-builder card.

4. Older employees will appreciate other benefits, such as private medical insurance, a dental plan or the chance to taper their retirement – along with the ability to add to their pension pot.

5. Instead of pushing your younger employees to save more for their pension, consider offering a blended savings solution, which they can use to meet their shorter-term needs.

ELEVEN

Effective Communications

It's good to talk

There's an old adage about some firms' management techniques being akin to mushroom farming: they keep workers in the dark, and feed them continuously on BS.

A key element of managing any workforce is to talk to your staff on a regular basis. The further flung your empire, the more important this becomes. You're heading off problems and misunderstandings before they develop, nipping unhelpful rumours in the bud, helping to cement your company's values and mission, and sharing the good news – as well as the less good news.

This communication has come a long way from the old-fashioned in-house newsletter that would land on employees' desks once a quarter… and end up in the bin shortly thereafter. Connecting with your teams, though, means understanding which channels work best for them, and that means segmenting your work-force. Put simply, post a letter to a Millennial and it will sit unopened on the stairs or the shelf in the hall forever. They'll be far happier receiving something they can read in their downtime, preferably on their smartphone or tablet.

Because of the way my company is structured – a relatively new entity, with thirteen offices around the country and more being added on a regular basis – we have put a lot of effort into our communications. The first step was to ask what our teams wanted from us. From the start, they called for more communications than they were already receiving, so they could 'feel' what's going on. They also wanted honesty in the communications they receive: who hasn't disregarded an in-house communication simply because it's obviously spin? In a 'post truth' world, an even higher value is placed on transparency and honesty. The Digital generation will really appreciate it, while the more cynical Analogues will spot BS a mile off.

In terms of communications channels, remember that this is the age of YouTube and podcasts, where you're far more likely to be viewed than read by younger people. Here are some things that have worked in my company:

- **Quarterly video updates.** In these, I am interviewed by a member of staff, who has previously collated topical questions from around the business. She does not let me avoid a question or provide weak answers. This gives me the chance to speak to everyone in the company, and for them to hear it from me directly.

- **An online magazine.** This contains news and videos from around the country, bringing together everyone in the business. This is driven by the Millennials, but we know from the feedback that we ask for (and receive) that employees in older generations appreciate it as well.

- **An internal Pulse quarterly survey.** This goes out to employees as an app on their phone, and asks them seven questions. The answers are anonymised, but I can see which branch they come from. If there are a number of disgruntled comments from one particular branch, I know there's a problem there that I need to address.

Trying these new communication methods has taught me that it's important not to hide behind the written word, but to embrace technology and put yourself out there honestly and openly.

Getting your pension messages across

Opposite you on your daily commute, a young woman is balancing a pile of official-looking papers on her lap and tapping into her smartphone. But she's not working. She is looking over her credit card bill, reviewing her monthly budget and checking her latest pension statement. One by one, she ticks off payments that she wants to look into and writes notes for herself.

If, like me, you are over the age of forty-five, the chances are that you have never done financial housekeeping while on your commute. According to a recent survey we conducted of 2,000 UK employees, between the ages of sixteen and sixty-five, just 12% of the over forty-fives have (Nelson, 2018). But among people under the age of forty-five, that figure is 37%. The younger cohort is much more likely to do their financial housekeeping on their lunch break (44% versus 20%).

This has major implications if you're trying to connect with your staff to tell them how their pension pot is faring. The majority of people do their financial housekeeping in the evening, at home, or on the weekend, but younger people are far more likely to do this task on the go, on the way to work or on a break. (Remember that the boundaries between work and home life are far blurrier for digital natives.)

If you have lots of staff members under the age of forty-five, this might affect the way you communicate with them. For example, you could send their pensions communications and statements to their homes and to their workplace, so they can access the information easily wherever they are. You could also send it in a format that is suitable for reading on a bus with no table, in a tunnel with no internet access, or in a noisy and busy environment.

These are questions of design and channel, not necessarily content. If you are looking to engage your staff with pensions, though, they are crucial to consider.

Making the pensions connection

It's important to encourage your employees to think ahead and make sure they are doing all the right things to secure their financial future. If you aren't sure how to do this effectively, here are three more findings from the Punter Southall Aspire survey (Nelson, 2018) that may influence how you communicate about pensions.

1. Words versus images?

In the survey, 46% of respondents over the age of forty-five wanted pension information to be conveyed in words. The proportion was lower – just 36% – among those under forty-five. Meanwhile, the younger group was much more interested in imagery than the older group (14% versus 4%). They were also keener on scenarios (26% versus 21%). Although in both instances, comments were made that they had not experienced either so were unsure how it would impact their interest. Both cohorts wanted information conveyed through numbers (24% among the younger group, 28% among the older group).

These findings suggest that it is sensible to make communications aimed at younger staff less wordy, and to include more imagery and scenarios that may resonate with them. If you're sending out one communication to your entire workforce, consider using a format that would allow people to choose how they want to access the information. For example, you might produce one basic piece of collateral and refer people who want more detail to an additional resource, such as a supplementary web page. Make sure everyone can access the information in a way that will resonate with them.

2. When to talk about pensions

Of the survey respondents, 84% (regardless of age) wanted to talk about their pensions when changes happen to their salary. And everyone wanted to hear about their pension when they started and left their job.

Younger workers (those under the age of forty-five) were much keener to talk about their pension at other times as well:

- At the point of recruitment: 71% of younger workers were in favour, versus 31% of older workers

- At the start and end of the tax year: 71% of younger workers were in favour, versus 35% of older workers

- During performance discussions or remuneration discussions with managers: 57% of younger workers were in favour compared to 39% of older workers

This indicates that there are many opportunities to bring up pensions with employees who are under the age of forty-five. This may be because respondents in this age bracket seem to be less sure about their pension situation (20% did not know how much they contribute, versus 13% of people over forty-five), so they are anxious for more information.

Don't be afraid of over-communicating: younger workers, in particular, are open to it. But think carefully about the best way to handle in-person conversations, as your managers might not be equipped or qualified to have them. If that is the case, consider asking your pension consultant to run workshops and one-to-one meetings with your staff.

3. What messaging to use

In the survey, people under the age of forty-five said that they would react to communication or marketing about pensions if it made them feel strong emotions, such as excitement (81%), guilt (39%) or fear (45%). Those who were older than forty-five claimed to be less likely to respond to strongly emotive material: 72% said they would respond to excitement, 26% to guilt and 32% to fear. Finally, 90% of employees from all age groups said that they would respond well to pensions communications that show they are receiving value for money.

In my experience, marketing that provokes emotion is always more successful than facts and figures. So, I recommend that you take the respondents at their word and make your pensions communications more emotional when targeting employees under forty-five. For example, when you talk about their future as pensioners, can you paint a picture of what life without enough money to live on might look like? Can you get them excited about living a retirement that they'll really enjoy? Test carefully how your older staff respond to more emotional content, too. The majority were receptive to pensions communications that stirred positive emotions, such as excitement. While many claimed to shy away from communications that relied on negative emotions, these often have the most powerful effect in marketing. It is worth seeing how these employees respond to it in reality.

Based on these findings, my company has developed a suite of thirty-second quickfire, light-hearted videos about their benefits to remind them of their value or that saving for a pension is a good idea. We send these videos to employees' smartphones. However, we still provide Boomer employees with a seriously worded, lengthy letter setting out all the reasons why they should save for their pension.

KEY POINTS

1. A key element of managing any workforce is to talk to your staff regularly. This allows you to head off problems and misunderstandings before they develop, nip unhelpful rumours in the bud, cement your company's values and mission, and share news.

2. However you communicate, be honest and open in what you say. Dishonesty will rapidly devalue any communication.

3. Digitals prefer videos and emails, but they don't open letters: the opposite of Analogues. Make sure everyone can access information in a way that will resonate with them.

4. There are many opportunities to bring up pensions with employees who are under the

age of forty-five: when they join your company, at the start or end of the tax year, and during performance discussions.

5. People under the age of forty-five say that they would react to communication about pensions if it made them feel strong emotions, such as excitement, guilt or fear. Those who are older claim to be less likely to respond to strongly emotive material, but it is worth testing how receptive they are in reality.

Conclusion: Getting the Balance Right

People's life expectancy is rising, while the numbers of younger (relatively footloose) people entering the workplace is shrinking. That can bring challenges and opportunities for your company. We've known about this demographic shift for some time now, but most companies have barely started to think about how they will actively manage a workplace where three (or more) generations will be expected to function smoothly together. Critically, too few experiences are being shared on how businesses can best enable people of all ages to complement each other's skills and assets, while ironing out generational differences in attitudes, priorities and approaches to work.

However, my research has found that some businesses are already managing intergenerational teams in ways that are giving them a serious competitive edge: not only in recruiting and retaining talented people but also in meeting the needs of their clients and customers.

No one pretends it's easy. Managing a business in today's fast-changing environment, where technology shifts can rapidly leave slow-footed businesses stranded, already poses a lot of challenges. It would be tempting to dismiss blending the generations as just another problem. In fact, in my experience, creating intergenerational teams can be the perfect way to future-proof your operation. Under one roof you can tap into the experiences, views, knowledge and creativity of a complete cross section of society.

In these circumstances (as in so many others), diversity is a strength, not a weakness. That has been proven conclusively in recent decades as the world of business has caught up with society and created equal opportunities for women and people from ethnic minorities. But creating a workplace where everyone can feel 'at home' – regardless of their background – is never going to be easy. I was reminded of this when my eldest daughter, who has just finished her master's degree in Physics, came home after getting her first job offer. To her, the company was perfect: coffee bars and sofas, roof gardens and buzzy workstations, and lots of people her own age to mingle with. While I can see all the Digitals in my company lapping that up, it did make me wonder if some of the older people in my team would have felt a bit like a dinosaur.

If we are to reap the benefits of intergenerational working, getting the right balance is essential – and that will mean making some compromises so that everyone can feel included in this brave new world we are creating. Most importantly, although we are all products of when and how we were brought up, we are all individuals. Understanding people as individuals, and then rewarding and supporting them accordingly, is the first step to bringing them together as seamless, motivated, high-functioning intergenerational teams.

Getting this right will involve some hard work. I spend far more time managing my people than my old bosses ever did. But your staff are your single biggest asset. Why wouldn't you want to maximise that asset?

Seven thoughts to leave you with

Here are seven key points to consider if you want to attract, develop and retain the most talented people – and build a sustainable, intergenerational workforce that will take your business forward.

1. **Age diversity is a strength.** All the research shows that having a mixed-age workforce makes for a more successful business. To make that happen, you need to build in working practices that accommodate different ethics and outlooks.

2. **Life's not just about work.** From the employee's perspective, these days it's all about work-life balance – for younger cohorts especially, but also for older workers whom you hope to retain. There's plenty you can do to make your company more attractive for a generation of people who work to live rather than live to work.

3. **Be flexible.** People of all ages want (and often need) to accommodate other pressures and activities in their lives. You might need to change some long-established practices, but the technology is now available to make it possible.

4. **There's no 'one size fits all'.** Old-style, broad-brush management techniques are no longer fit for purpose. Everyone is an individual – with different personal needs and aspirations – and it's up to you to know what these are and develop a rewards and benefits structure that works for them.

5. **Don't assume.** To recruit the best people, don't make assumptions about who can bring something special to your business. Age should never be a barrier – at either end of the spectrum – and neither should work gaps or experience in different spheres.

6. **Keep communicating with your people.** Let them know what you are thinking, and listen to what they want to say to you. Remember, this might be best achieved by using different communication channels.

7. **Give your people opportunities to learn.** Keep your team constantly learning, growing and developing new skills: the jobs they do now may soon be obsolete, but you'll still want them in your business.

Appendix: The Money Charity

I am passionate about building a more financially informed and secure society, and my business is constantly developing new ways to transform people's financial future. To support these aims, we have developed a partnership with The Money Charity, an organisation that can reach a broader cross section of society with education, information and advice on money matters.

I will donate 100% of the proceeds from this book to The Money Charity.

The Money Charity is the UK's financial capability charity. They believe that being on top of your money means you are more in control of your life, your finances and your debts, reducing stress and hardship.

It increases your wellbeing, helps you achieve your goals and live a happier, more positive life.

Their vision is for everyone to be on top of their money as part of everyday life. They empower people across the UK to build the skills, knowledge, attitudes and behaviours to make the most of their money throughout their lives.

They achieve this by developing and delivering products and services which provide education, information and advice on money matters in an appropriate way for young people and adults.

They work with all parts of the financial services industry to improve practice and outcomes for their consumers.

They influence and inform policymakers, the media, the industry and public attitudes to support their vision, purpose and delivery.

www.themoneycharity.org.uk

References

Angeloni, S. & Borgonovi, E., 2016. An ageing world and the challenges for a model of sustainable social change. *Journal of Management Development*, 35(4), pp. 464–485.

Armstrong-Stassen, M. & Schlosser, F., 2008. Benefits of a supportive development climate for older workers. *Journal of Managerial Psychology*, 23(4), pp. 419–437.

Backes-Gellner, U. & Veen, S., 2013. Positive effects of aging and age diversity in innovative companies: large-scale empirical evidence on company productivity. *Human Resource Management Journal*, 23(3), pp. 279–295.

Barrett, J. & Bourke, J., 2013. Managing for inclusion: engagement with an aging workforce. *Employment Relations Record*, 13(1), pp. 13–24.

Bersin, J. & Chamorro-Premuzic, T., 2018. 4 Ways to Create a Learning Culture on Your Team. Harvard Business Review [Online] www.hbr.org/2018/07/4-ways-to-create-a-learning-culture-on-your-team [Accessed 2 Aug 2019].

BITC, 2019a. *Agile Working*. [Online] Available at: https://age.bitc.org.uk/issues/Agileflexibleworking [Accessed 23 April 2019].

BITC, 2019b. *Dispelling Common Myths*. [Online] Available at: www.bitc.org.uk/sites/default/files/myth_buster_factsheet.pdf [Accessed 21 June 2019].

BITC, 2019c. Six Tips to Motivate Millennials. [Online] https://age.bitc.org.uk/sites/default/files/motivating_millenials_-_6_tips.pdf [Accessed 2 Aug 2019].

Carers UK, 2019. *State of Caring Survey 2019*. [Online] Available at: www.carersuk.org/news-and-campaigns/state-of-caring-survey-2019 [Accessed 28 May 2019].

CBI, 2018. Half of young people do not feel prepared for world of work. [Online] www.cbi.org.uk/media-centre/articles/half-of-young-people-do-not-feel-prepared-for-world-of-work-cbi-accenture-hays-survey/ [Accessed 2 Aug 2019].

Centre for Ageing Better, 2018. *Impact Report 2017–2018*. London: Centre for Ageing Better. [Online] www.ageing-better.org.uk/sites/default/files/2018-09/Becoming-age-friendly-employer.pdf [Accessed 1 Aug 2019].

CIPD, 2014. *Managing an Age-Diverse Workforce: Employer and Employee Views*. London: Chartered Institute of Personnel and Development.

CIPD, 2019. Older workers and women returners emerge as winners from jobs boom [Online] www.cipd.co.uk/about/media/press/older-workers-winners-jobs-boom [Accessed 1 Aug 2019].

Conley, C., 2018. *What Baby Boomers Can Learn from Millennials at Work – and Vice Versa*. TED talk. [Online] Available at: www.ted.com/talks/chip_conley_what_baby_boomers_can_learn_from_millennials_at_work_and_vice_versa?language=en [Accessed 28 March 2019].

Cridland, J., 2017. *Independent Review of the State Pension Age; Smoothing the Transition*. London: Her Majesty's Stationery Office.

Dearing, R., 1997. *The National Committee of Inquiry into Higher Education*. London: Her Majesty's Stationery Office.

Deloitte, 2017. *The 2017 Deloitte Millennial Survey*. London: Deloitte Touche Tohmatsu.

Deloitte, 2017. *Apprehensive Millennials: Seeking Stability and Opportunities in an Uncertain World*. London: Deloitte Touche Tohmatsu.

DiversityQ, 2018. Strategies for diversity: Q&A with Sarah Kaiser from Fujitsu. [Online] Available at: https://diversityq.com/strategies-for-diversity-with-sarah-kaiser-fujitsu-1003827 [Accessed 6 Aug 2019].

DTI, 2006. *The Employment Equality (Age) Regulations 2006*. [Online] Available at: www.legislation.gov.uk/uksi/2006/1031/contents/made [Accessed 9 March 2019].

Edmans, A., 2012. The link between job satisfaction and firm value, with implications for corporate social responsibility. *Academy of Management Perspectives*, 26(4), pp. 1–19.

Forbes, 2019. Are returnships the key to relaunching your career? [Online] Available at: www.forbes.com/sites/jasonwingard/2019/02/13/

are-returnships-the-key-to-relaunching-your-career/#1ffbc95e3cdf [Accessed 6 Aug 2019].

Grabmeler, J., 2019. Creativity is not just for the young, study finds. *Ohio State News*, 26 April. [Online] Available at: https://news.osu.edu/creativity-is-not-just-for-the-young-study-finds [Accessed 21 June 2019].

Gratton, L. & Scott, A., 2016. *The 100 Year Life; Living and Working in an Age of Longevity*. London, UK: Bloomsbury Information.

Grubb, V., 2017. *Clash of the Generations; Managing the New Workplace Reality*. New Jersey: John Wiley & Sons.

Hadfield, W., 2019. BNY Mellon shelves tighter work-at-home rules after uproar. *Bloomberg*, 7 March. [Online] Available at: www.bloomberg.com/news/articles/2019-03-07/bny-mellon-shelves-tighter-work-at-home-rules-after-staff-uproar [Accessed 7 March 2019].

Hall, S. R. K. & Williams, R., 2019. *The Perennials: The Future of Ageing*. London: Ipsos Group.

Hess, T., Auman, C., Colcombe, S. & Rahhal, T., 2003. The impact of stereotype threat on age differences in memory performance. *The Journals of Gerontology*, 58(1), pp. 3–11.

Hill, A., 2019. Number of over-70s still in work more than doubles in a decade. *Guardian*, 27 May. [Online] Available at: www.theguardian.com/money/2019/may/27/number-of-over-70s-still-in-work-more-than-doubles-in-a-decade [Accessed 21 June 2019].

HMRC, 2014. *Taxation of Pensions Act 2014*. [Online] Available at: www.legislation.gov.uk/ukpga/2014/30/contents/enacted [Accessed 9 March 2019].

Horn, J, 1965. A rationale and test for the number of factors in factor analysis. *Psychometrika*, Volume 30, Issue 2, pp 179–185.

Hughes, K., 2018. Number of people retiring after age 70 doubles since 2010. *Independent*, 21 March [Online] Available at: www.independent.co.uk/money/spend-save/retirement-late-number-age-70-pension-work-longer-a8266461.html [Accessed 21 March 2019].

Kay, L., 2017. More young people are volunteering, says nfpSynergy research. *Third Sector*, 28 September. [Online] Available at: www.thirdsector.co.uk/young-people-volunteering-says-nfpsynergy-research/volunteering/article/1445878 [Accessed 21 June 2019].

Kooij, D., Jansen, P., Dikkers, J. & de Lange, A., 2010. The influence of age on the associations between HR practices and both affective commitment and job satisfaction. *Journal of Organizational Behaviour*, 31(8), pp. 1111–1136.

Lain, D. & Loretto, W., 2016. Managing employees beyond age 65: from the margins to the mainstream? *Employee Relations*, 38(5), pp. 646–664.

Larkin, N., 2019. *Age Diversity: How to Engage Different Age Groups in Your Workplace.* [Online] Available at: www.cv-library.co.uk/recruitment-insight/engage-different-age-groups-your-workplace [Accessed 21 June 2019].

Lefkowitz, R., Spar, B., Dye, C. & Pate, D., 2018. *The Rise and Responsibility of Talent Development in the New Labor Market.* Sunnyvale: LinkedIn.

Manorek, K., 2019. *How to Reach Diverse Learners in the Workplace.* [Online] Available at: www.td.org/insights/how-to-reach-diverse-learners-in-the-workplace [Accessed 13 June 2019].

Mercer, 2017. *Mercer's Global Talents Survey 2017.* New York: Mercer LLC.

NAO, 2018. Tackling problem debt; our vision is to help the nation spend wisely. London: National Audit Office.

Nelson, J., 2018. *It's Time to Change.* London: Punter Southall Aspire.

NIACE, 2015. Mid Life Career Review; Pilot Project Outcomes: Phases 1, 2, and 3 (2013–2015). Leicester: National Institute of Adult Continuing Education.

Ofcom, 2018. A Decade of Digital Dependency, London, UK [Online] www.ofcom.org.uk/about-ofcom/latest/features-and-news/decade-of-digital-dependency [Accessed 2 Aug 2019].

ONS, 2015. *How Has Life Expectancy Changed over Time?* [Online] Available at: www.ons.gov.uk/people populationandcommunity/birthsdeathsandmarriages/ lifeexpectancies/articles/howhaslifeexpectancy changedovertime/2015-09-09 [Accessed 6 June 2019].

ONS, 2016. Results 2014 based national population projections reference volume, UK [online] Available at: www.ons.gov.uk/peoplepopulationandcommunity/ populationandmigration/populationprojections/ compendium/nationalpopulationprojections/2014 basedreferencevolumeseriespp2/chapter4mortality-2014basednationalpopulationprojectionsreferencev-olume [Accessed 1 Aug 2019].

ONS, 2017. Overview of the UK population, UK. [Online] Available at: www.ons.gov.uk/peoplepopulationand community/populationandmigration/population estimates/articles/overviewoftheukpopulation/ mar2017#consequences-of-these-population-changes [Accessed 1 Aug 2019].

ONS, 2018. *Home Business, Industry and Trade IT and Internet Industry Internet Users, UK.* [Online] Available at: www.ons.gov.uk/businessindustryandtrade/ itandinternetindustry/bulletins/internetusers/2018 [Accessed 28 March 2019].

Parliament UK, 2012. Education: Historical statistics [Online] Available at: https://researchbriefings.files. parliament.uk/documents/SN04252/SN04252.pdf [Accessed 1 Aug 2019].

Parry, E. & Urwin, P., 2017. The evidence base for generational differences: where do we go from here? *Work, Aging & Retirement,* 3(2), pp. 140–148.

Patrickson, M. & Ranzijn, R., 2004. Bounded choices in work and retirement in Australia. *Employee Relations,* 26(4), pp. 422–432.

Pension Policy Institute, 2016. DB Today and Tomorrow [online] Available at: https://www.pensionspolicy institute.org.uk/media/1355/201612-bn86-db-today- and-tomorrow.pdf [Accessed 1 Aug 2019].

Pew Research Centre, 2010. *Millennials: Confident, Connected and Open to Change.* [Online] Available at: www.pewsocialtrends.org/2010/02/24/millennials- confident-connected-open-to-change [Accessed 21 June 2019].

Posthuma, R. & Campion, M., 2009. Age stereotypes in the workplace: common stereotypes, moderators and future research directions. *Journal of Management*, 35(1), pp. 185–227.

Price Waterhouse Cooper, 2013. NextGen: A global generational study: Evolving talent strategy to match the new workforce reality. London: PricewaterhouseCoopers International Limited.

Radford, K. & Chapman, G., 2015. Are all workers influenced to stay by similar factors or should different retention strategies be implemented: comparing younger and older aged care-workers in Australia. *Australian Bulletin of Labour*, 41(1), pp. 58–81.

Randstad, 2019. *86% of Hong Kongers Prefer Their Managers to be Older.* [Online] Available at: www.randstad.com.hk/about-us/news/86-of-hongkongers-prefer-their-managers-to-be-older/?utm_source=email&utm_medium=pr&utm_campaign=workmonitor2018 [Accessed 28 March 2019].

Schloegel, U., Stegmann, S., van Dick, R. & Maedche, A., 2018. Age stereotypes in distributed software development: the impact of culture on age-related performance expectations. *Information and Software Technology*, 97, pp. 146–162.

Smith, S. & Galbraith, Q., 2012. Motivating Millennials: improving practice in recruiting, retaining and motivating younger library staff. *Journal of Academic Librarianship*, 38(3), pp. 135–144.

Swinson, Jo (joswinson) "Feel like sending a fax to @BNYMellon to tell them its 2019...maybe a carrier pigeon?" Twitter 6 March 2019, 12:14pm.

TANR, 2019. The Age of No Retirement [Online] Available at: www.ageofnoretirement.org/ [Accessed 2 Aug 2019].

Twenge, J., 2016. Do Millennials have lesser work ethic? The actual science from national survey data over time. *Psychology Today*, 24 February. [Online] Available at: www.psychologytoday.com/ca/blog/our-changing-culture/201602/do-millennials-have-lesser-work-ethic [Accessed 23 April 2019].

Wegge, J., Jungmann, F., Liebermann, S., Shemla, M., Ries, B.C., Diestel, S. & Schmidt, K.H., 2012. What makes age-diverse teams effective? Results from a six-year research program. *Work*, 41, pp. 5145–5151.

Williams, M., 2015. Being trusted: how team generation age diversity promotes and undermines trust in cross-boundary relationships. *Journal of Organisational Behaviour*, 37(3), pp. 346–373.

World Economic Forum, 2019. *Japan's Workforce Will Be 20% Smaller by 2040*. [Online] Available at: www.weforum.org/agenda/2019/02/japan-s-workforce-will-shrink-20-by-2040 [Accessed 21 June 2019].

The Author

Steve Butler is a Chartered Manager and Fellow of the Chartered Management Institute. He gained his master's in business administration from Southampton, Solent University and is currently researching for his doctorate in business administration at Winchester University, Centre for Responsible Management. He is a regular writer and speaker on intergenerational working, retirement and older worker business management issues. He is also passionate about helping corporates and individuals become more financially informed.

As a newly promoted manager at the age of twenty-six, Steve was put in charge of his first team of eight investment specialists at Scottish Widows. There he overcame the challenges of managing older, more experienced workers and the complexities of managing remote team members across the UK. At age thirty-two, he established his own technology business with a small age-diverse team of employees. This is now part of Punter Southall Aspire, a national retirement savings business. As Chief Executive, Steve is building innovative technology-led solutions to help corporates and individuals manage their employee benefits and retirement savings.

Steve lives in Richmond with his wife and their family of seven children and stepchildren. Aged between seventeen and twenty-two, they provide him with an array of perspectives on how individuals in the upcoming Generation Z are approaching the workplace. He believes that the intergenerational conflict is only set to get worse as these digital natives begin working alongside his more mature colleagues.

Steve was born in 1970, which makes him an early member of Generation X. Thanks to his career in technology and his large family, he is a firm Digital sympathiser.

⊕ www.managethegap.com

in www.linkedin.com/in/stevenbutler/

⊕ www.psaspire.com